▸TARGETED◂

DAVID GIDEON

Targeted © 2021 David Gideon

All rights reserved. No part of this publication may be reproduced, distributed, or transmitted in any form or by any means, including photocopying, recording, or other electronic or mechanical methods, without the prior written permission of the publisher, except in the case brief quotations embodied in critical reviews and other noncommercial uses permitted by copyright law.

ISBN:
Paperback   978-1-63945-267-5
E-book   978-1-63945-268-2

The views expressed in this book are solely those of the author and do not necessarily reflect the views of the publisher, and the publisher hereby disclaims any responsibility for them.

Writers' Branding
1800-608-6550
www.writersbranding.com
orders@writersbranding.com

CONTENTS

Dedication v
Preface vii
Introduction xi

PART ONE

- Chapter One – 1
  The Beginning at Data Systems Corp Early Years -
  Before I Met That Horrific Bully 1

- Chapter Two – 7
  Data Systems-Where I Met My Worst Nightmare 7
  Serenity Prayer 7
  House Warming Party – Invite from a friend 23
  Following me home after work 25
  Golf Outing - 2005 27
  The Other Woman 30
  Temporary Insanity 31
  Temporary Leave of Absence from the Office 32
  Back in the Office 33
  Leaving Data Systems Corporation – Position Outsourced to India .. 36

- Chapter Three - 39
  After Data Systems 39
  My Friend Rick – after we are both out of Data Systems 41
  Visit's in Little Rock 43

- Chapter Four - 49
  New Contract in Pittsburgh PA 49
  Meeting with my worst nightmare at a new job location 50
  Building Security 52
  Escorted out of the building by security 53
  Visit from our senior director of HR 56
  A Close Encounter 57
  Bully's final day in building 59

- Chapter Five - 65
  My final days in Wexford 65
  Being Blown Away 67

- Chapter Six – 71
  What should I have done? 71
  Visits in Little Rock (2009 - 2012) 73
  Visits in Pittsburgh (October 15, 2012 – January 25, 2013) 75

- Chapter Seven – 79
  Helping out where I can 79

- Chapter Eight - 85
  A New and Promising Future 85

Our Anti-Bully Crusade 85
  - Chapter Nine – 89
  The real question is WHY? 89

- Chapter Ten - 93
  Grace and Forgiveness 93

TARGETED

PART TWO

Section I
   Legal Action 103

Section II 105
   Should and Should Not.. 105
   In the Workplace - What Should the Witnesses Do?............................ 105
   In the Work Place - What Should You
   (The Target) Focus On... 106
   In School   What Should the Witnesses Do 108
   In School - What Should You (The Target) Focus On 109

Section III 111
   Some Anti-Bully Websites for help and
   support in the Workplace 111
   For Children:.. 113

DEDICATION

I would like to dedicate this book to all those men and women who find themselves in the midst of a Work Place Bully and are getting unnecessarily stressed out, which is directly caused from the bully. Sometimes the harder way (thinking positive and not going postal) is the best solution.

I would like to thank my wife, Rachel, who has been very supportive of me and all the work I have been doing in my anti-bully crusade over the last several years.

To all children who find themselves being tormented by Bullies, harassed in school and on the playground. No matter how hard it gets, just remember one thing. YOU ARE NOT ALONE, AND DON'T EVER BE AFRAID TO ASK FOR HELP.

PREFACE

Please note that the names of all those involved, including the Bully, have all been changed to protect both the innocent and the guilty.

Please note that I am not looking for sympathy from this book. Explaining my story doesn't just help me to bring closure as to what had happened to me, but it also describes as to how one very aggressive bully can manipulate an entire department in a working environment with the sole intention to turn someone's life upside down and, in the process, actually destroy someone's career. I want others to realize and understand just how someone with bad intentions can come into their lives and create such a hostile working environment. The bully I'm about to discuss actually pulled everyone's strings and ultimately created a hostile working environment where bullying was allowed to continue. Management didn't know how to handle the situation, so they looked the other way every time the bully assaulted me.

Maybe there's someone in your workplace who is doing something similar. What will you do if you run across a bully in your workplace? What are the ethic policies in your workplace? What is the law in the state where you are working that deal with bullies in the workplace?

Well, I will attempt to answer these questions while telling my story. I have asked myself "why me?" several times.

My story is true and is also very hard to believe. The person who has targeted me did a lot of things in that. When I told others, they would question the bully. "Did you really do that? I just can't believe it." The bully would just look at them with a smile and walk away.

After my last horrific experience in Pittsburgh, Pennsylvania, I went down a very long road of depression and despair. During that time, I received a lot of support from my family and friends at the Church. Even in a depressed state, I eventually came up with ideas of helping others who find themselves in similar situations. I feel, now at age 67, that this is the best way for me to spend my early retirement years.

After I lost my job as a Tandem Consultant in Pittsburgh Pennsylvania, I was stunned, and left with many unpaid bills, including a new Android phone, which I had just purchased during the best Christmas I had in a very long while.

In February 2013, an idea had suddenly popped into my head about creating anti-bully apps. I also had noticed that at that time, there wasn't anything like it available on the android market. Since I had over 25 years of experience as a developer, I figured that I'm smart enough to create such an application.

After what happened to me, which was from the same person who had begun his reign of terror on me back when I first met and worked with him at Data Systems Corporation in 2005, I figured that I had two choices. One Positive and one negative idea came to mind.

I chose the positive direction, which is to help others who find themselves being bullied. I don't ever want what had happened to me to ever happen to anyone else.

The most difficult thing I ever had to do is work towards a path of forgiveness to that bully who had wreaked havoc in my life and had destroyed my reputation and career.

The minister from my church gave me a copy of the book, Grace and Forgiveness by John and Carol Arnott.

They wrote "We all have a story to tell. There will be readers who have been abused, lied about, betrayed, walked over, taken advantage of, hurt by their closest friend, let down by an authority figure – the list is endless. John and Carol give illustrations and reasons for forgiving that will want you to forgive in a way you never dreamed possible. The greater the suffering, the greater the anointing. If you have suffering more than most then you have a promise of Blessing that is greater than that which is promised to those who have not been hurt as you have."

INTRODUCTION

Many of us have been bullied at times, especially as a youngster in school. Some of us learned at such early ages as to how to deal with such harassment. As one matures to adulthood, one builds a self-defense mechanism where one can have an aura about themselves enough to where one is not thought of as an easy victim (target) of bullies.

Today we realize that bullying actually maims and even kills. Over four thousand children commit suicide every year, and a lot of those suicides are a direct result from bullying (statistic taken from CBC web site).

When someone goes postal in the workplace or our schools, bullying is usually the culprit somewhere in the perpetrator's life.

No one likes being bullied, and no one likes to admit that bullying even exists, but it does.

When I was young, I had several friends. Some were in school, and some were in extracurricular activities I participated in, which was usually Boy Scouts. When a bully or group of bullies began harassing me, my friends became onlookers and was hoping that the bully wouldn't start in on them.

It seemed that I was always an easy target of a bully. During these early times, I never learned how to fend for myself and as a result of all the bullying; I had low self- esteem and low self-confidence.

I would run home crying to my Mom and Dad. Mom said that I should turn the other cheek, and my Dad would usually say "why do these kids have to fight?" Then he would quietly go over and visit the bully's parents.

I never once was shown how to fend for myself, and usually, after my father visited those parents, the bullying just got worse the next day.

The earliest time I remember myself being bullied was when I was six years old. And, to my dismay, I've been bullied all my life.

My goal for this book is to first cover my latest experiences of being deliberately targeted and bullied by a very aggressive workplace bully for over the last twenty plus years of my life.

As I mentioned earlier, the names of all those involved, including the Bully, have all been changed to protect both the innocent and the guilty.

I'm going to attempt to explain in detail as to what life was like during employment at Data Systems Corporation and how this horrific bully had kept tabs of me over the years after I left the company in August 2007.

This guy simply won't leave me alone. Why is that? What reason would anyone want to do such an aggressive form of harassment on another human being? I tell others this story, but they usually find it very hard to believe.

Whenever you use the word, "bully" people normally think of kids in school. Not too many people are really familiar with this form of bullying, which is a very aggressive form of harassment performed by adults.

Whenever I'm being bullied, I really feel alone. My wife and family don't understand what I was going through in each day at work. The pain and anguish are unbelievable. During my last assault with this guy (2012 – 2013), I didn't say anything to anybody until it was too late.

As the old saying goes, it takes two to tango. Whenever he had assaulted me, he made it appear that I (his target) was the main problem. He made it appear that I just don't know how to get along with others.

I'm the one who had to go. The bully wins out, and Management goes along with him (path of least resistance). Everyone is happy except for the Target (Me) who ultimately gets screwed.

What I mean by "serial bully" is someone who keeps track of his / her target and assaults his / her target whenever and wherever he can. In this case, after I left Data Systems, he continued with harassing me when I worked in Little Rock Arkansas (2009 - 2012) and at Pittsburgh PA where I started a new position in 2012. That Bully is a bully to the nth degree.

The second part of this book will focus mainly on what you can do if you a target or another innocent bystander (from some lessons learned). I will be discussing what the person being targeted and what the bystanders should do when they are in the presence of a bully. This advice had come to me from an assortment of material that I read in books and from articles I found on the internet.

PART ONE

This is my personal story about my experiences of being bullied by the same very horrible workplace bully for over the last umpteen years (since 2005).

- CHAPTER ONE -

The Beginning at Data Systems Corp Early Years - Before I Met That Horrific Bully

It all began when I was working for Data Systems Corporation, located in Wilmington DE, after over four years of hard work in what most people would consider being a hostile working environment. The old saying that "the squeaky wheel gets the most oil" was the motto by many of the employees at that company. There were rules, but just the same, if you were the most outspoken person in the group, you usually got your own way.

When I was first interviewed there, all I saw was what appeared to be a great group of people, a beautiful park to take walks in during lunch, the gym downstairs, and most of all, a substantial increase in income if I accepted the position.

But looks can be deceiving. If I knew back then what I know now, I most likely would not have taken that position. What I saw looking in from the outside was much different than what I saw when looking in from the inside. We all had to work very hard, under very harsh scrutiny and very tight schedules. It got to the point where we all were worrying about losing our jobs on a daily basis.

My first task was to design, develop, and eventually implement a temporary process which they had to have in place before their new Debit Card System could ever go live.

With my knowledge and experience of COBOL (Common Business Oriented Language) application development and Tandem computer systems, this seemed like a fairly simple task. I was given a three-month timeline to get a functional process in place, and I felt that I could meet their timeline.

Every day senior management had been leaning back and forth as to whether or not if our new system was even going to become a reality. We all knew that if they had decided against it, we would all find ourselves back in the unemployment line. But that didn't happen. Instead, they had decided to move forward with this project and to plan its implementation shortly after the year 2000 changes had been implemented.

That was great, and everyone felt more secure with their jobs. Besides, working on the temporary embossing process, I was also responsible for other processes such as some of the Tandem reporting processes. We were always under a certain amount of pressure to meet our schedules, so we all worked late to get everything running smoothly.

Then one day, it happened. For some reason, my manager was immediately terminated and that there was someone else coming on site to take over this project and see it through to its final implementation.

Harley arrived, and all during this changeover, we all began worrying about our future with the company once again. Harley was a senior manager, so he brought in someone else to take over my old manager's position. Dick came on board, and Harley called each one of us on the team into his office for a personal meeting with the two of them to get an idea as to how we each could be the best fit into their new department they were forming.

After the meetings, Harley then began to hire a group of senior consultants, and we all suddenly found ourselves (employees) competing with these so-called experts. During that time, it appeared that the consultants had management's ear, and we employees found ourselves at their mercy.

Most of us full-time employees there were considered to be inexperienced during this time. And we were. Many of us didn't really know anything about SQL or how to embed it in our COBOL code. But, the consultants did. The only thing was that many of them were bullies in their own right.

For quite a while, the daily competition in the office was fierce. Several consultants had worked on prolonging their contracts by making it appear that they were more qualified to do our jobs than we were. These consultants would make us look bad whenever possible. One consultant, working in my software, actually tried to set me up, by causing issues with my code.

My personality usually put me on the defensive. When that happened, several issues surfaced where I was the blame. When I questioned my own capabilities, my reputation had become tarnished. For quite a while I thought I was going to be fired, but that ultimately didn't happen. Harley had enough with some of the consultants because they were trying to take over the project.

Harley came in one day and had most of the consultants in our team immediately terminated. After that, only a hand full of consultants had remained and stayed on for a little while longer. There was one hotshot consultant, Johnny, who had caused a lot of tension in the office, and who also had gotten me in trouble several times with my manager.

Even with my reputation of having low self-esteem and low self-confidence, I was to take over everything that Johnny was responsible for. Though several people didn't agree with this decision, I still ended up stepping up to the plate and doing his job as well as mine.

There were times when the consultants would question our work. Some teammates were able to address this swiftly, and with them, enough confidence to make them in the right. Some of the consultants would put down some of the employees, I inclusive, stating that some of us didn't belong there working on such a high-profile project.

Then, Dick hired a developer, Joana, to assume a management role. We all knew Joana from before as a developer, but we just weren't sure how she would do as a manager. She was to report directly to him and oversee our work. One thing we discovered with Joana is that once there were issues between employees in her department, she would work on getting rid of it by turning the employees over (transferring) to another manager.

For quite a while I was doing fine handling on-call support, meeting deadlines, etc. on my own but Harley had different plans for me. He brought in someone else, Arash, to assist me in what I was doing. I immediately began showing him what I was doing, and while doing that, I realized that he could also be somewhat of a bully when he wants to be.

To cover up his lack of knowledge on something, he would stomp his feet, go running to Joana, the Manager of our department, and work at making me feel that I was the person who was the real problem.

Arash was born and raised in Iraq and seemed to have two-sided personality. A spiritual side and a non-spiritual bully side. He used the bully side whenever he felt threatened or questioned about anything.

One day, several of us went out to lunch together. On the way to the restaurant, while we were in a traffic jam, there was an irate driver behind us honking his horn. Then while the other car was slowly passing us, Arash pulled his seat belt behind him, then shifted to the left, and giving a horrific stare in kind of a gawking fashion which took the other driver by complete surprise. We asked him where he learned how to do that, and he said that his father taught him.

This is my first experience of the type of mental bullying harassment that I would someday have to put up with what would become my absolute worst nightmare.

It seemed that every project we had worked on included a lot of arguing between the two of us. Joana could only put up with this behavior only so much until finally; each of us were being transferred into new departments. Arash was promoted to an architect position and relocated over to a different building, and I made a lateral move upstairs as a developer to the End of Day department. Joana informed me that I would be maintaining the other side of the Card Management and Authorization system, which was supported by EOD.

I wrote many of the Tandem Card Embossing Management processes during my first four years with the company (called the front end) which delivered files over to the UNIX side for final processing and delivery to the customers.

- CHAPTER TWO -

Data Systems-Where I Met My Worst Nightmare

"God grant me the serenity to accept the things I cannot change; Courage to change the things I can, and wisdom to know the difference."

Serenity Prayer

I recited this to myself each day this clown was bullying me. That helped me feel that I really wasn't alone.

The department I moved to was the UNIX platform (considered the back end of our process). My new boss, Eric, had a system in place where more than one person knew each part of the End of Day system. It was like a buddy system. He felt that if I or someone else, God forbid, ever got hit by a bus, then there would always be someone else available who could step up to the plate and take over supporting what needed to be supported.

This was where I first met Maurice, who quickly became my good friend and colleague. We worked together on several projects. I showed him the ropes on the Tandem system, and he showed me how to do things on the UNIX platform. During that time, on-call support was on a rotation bass for the EOD system. But if there were any issues relating to the Card Embossing system, I was called. Maurice, my backup, was also called to listen in on the conference call, so that he could eventually be able to handle any future application support issues as needed.

Maurice was very nice to me and even demonstrated that he had a great sense of humor. He liked to tell jokes and play little innocent pranks. There was one time when I went on a two-week vacation, and when I returned, my office cube was decorated with huge "Welcome Back" posters and a lot of other stuff geared to put a real smile on my face. I later found out that he talked everyone in the department into helping him in this endeavor.

Before I continue, I'll mention that I added in some illustrations to the following pages wherever specifically the bully was mentioned, both when he acted like my friend, or my enemy (a picture is worth a thousand words). I thought this was a great way to really explain what I actually went through.

As friends, we always enjoyed taking a walk together in the nearby Belleview State Park, which was situated next door to our office. The park was actually the old DuPont residence, which had been donated by the family to the State of Delaware.

I would say that we did this almost daily. It was great exercise and an excellent stress reliever.

The following illustration shows Maurice and I walking in the park as great friends, which we were during that time.

This was a great place to take a break and relax while working on such software that always seemed to have with it a high amount of visibility. There was always a certain amount of pressure in the office. There was a "zero" tolerance, where if anyone had ever made any of those mistakes, they would be terminated immediately and escorted out of the building. Our daily walks in the park, visiting the horses that resided there in the stables, and walking on the old DuPont dirt race track, gave us a great feeling of temporary relaxation.

Maurice always walked slightly, hunched over while swinging his right arm. I'm only mentioning this now to prepare you what lies ahead for me. This, what looked to be a bad habit, was actually part of his preparation to aggressively bully me.

We determined that our walk from the office door, once around the race track, and the walk back to the office, was actually around a two-mile walk, making it an excellent daily exercise.

During our walks, we would discuss our personal lives, how things were going and other aspects of our professional life at Data Systems.

He had learned about my questionable reputation from others who were still working there and were familiar with those rumors. The most damaging story was with my work on the Card Embossing program. To set the record straight, the following is what really happened:

On July 1997, I first began working at Data Systems Corporation. I was told by my new Manager to write a simple Temporary program to generate a type of Debit card for them. This was the last thing they needed to move their entire new system into Production. The general plan was to put a newer, more robust process in place after everything was running smoothly.

Then suddenly there was a change in management. My Boss was fired, and we suddenly found ourselves working under new management. As I mentioned earlier, our new boss had decided that we needed to create a more competitive workplace. We found ourselves working in an environment where half of the team was employees, and the other half was made up of a bunch of hotshot Consultants.

After the smoke cleared, I was called into a special meeting with senior management on discussing the current Card Embossing process. The managers and new Senior Consultants wanted me to simply modify my current process to handle all types of card processing. This was a new management decision change.

During the meeting, I was ordered not to tell anybody else what I was instructed to do. So, I made the changes and got everything working correctly as discussed at that meeting.

It wasn't the most excellent system, but it was basically just what they had asked for. I delivered the modified program on schedule, and after fixing a few bugs, it had been running in production for over the last twenty plus years.

TARGETED

I have been criticized for it being a poorly written process ever since its original implementation in the year 2000. I am personally responsible for having a system which to date has been running successfully for all these years.

Because of this program's poor reputation, I have never received any accommodations for it or anything else. I just have the personal gratification that I did something successfully and that it has lasted as long as it has. This is a temporary process that I made permanent, which had also had made a lot of money for Data Systems.

Maurice and I had continued our daily walks in the park together. We enjoyed our times going out and taking a nice break from our rigid and sometimes stressful schedules. We even went shopping together during the holidays. It was a great time.

I remember a couple of times while shopping together, Maurice had suggested a few items which were on sale. We went 50/50 on the purchased a new set of binoculars with a built-in camera for our boss, Eric.

Another instance is when Maurice had suggested a TV for my Wife. It was on sale for only $50 bucks. I thought it would be great, and I didn't stop to think that the screen was only fifteen inches and that my Wife wouldn't really appreciate it.

Maurice had also suggested that we each purchase a reflector telescope which was also on sale. He eventually returned his, but I kept mine because of my interest in learning astronomy.

Over the years, I eventually got rid of both the small TV and the scope.

Several years went by until one day in the park; Maurice began discussing something to me, which took me by complete surprise. Again, whenever I tell this story to others, they just look at me with disbelief. With everything, Maurice had done, and with the reactions

I've received from others, I actually feel like I've been living in some kind of Stephen King novel.

On one bright sunny day while walking in the park Maurice turned to me and said "I'm going to have to begin doing something to you, and for that I'm sorry. It's that I'm concerned with my current position at work and that I want to make sure that my job is secure."

He evidently saw something in the future that I didn't see. He also gave me a brief insight as to just who and what he really was.

In the office, he usually walked hunched over with his right arm swinging across the front of him. He also mentioned to me that he has a condition with his eyes where he can protrude the eyeball out a bit. He said that it's all an act to mess with people's heads in the office.

As I mentioned before, he was trying to prepare me for what was about to happen to me. I wish I paid more attention to what he was actually telling me. Remembering this day has helped me from going completely insane. But when his entire BS began, I was taken completely off guard and everything he had originally told me on that day just went right out the window.

The next day I came into the office and began doing my morning system checks and was getting ready to go down to the cafeteria for my usual breakfast sandwich and coffee.

Before I left, Maurice stopped by my cube and said to me that he wanted to discuss something with me in private. So, we both went down stairs together to the cafeteria got our breakfast and found an area where we could sit down and have some privacy.

He told me that he had heard that I was talking about him behind his back and to please stop it. That he didn't like it. I assured him that I was not, nor would I ever do anything like that. I asked him where he was getting this information from. He wouldn't tell me. He then threatened me and told me again never to do it again (as if he didn't believe me).

Then later that same day, I had to discuss some work with another member of our staff (Jim).

I walked around the corner, and there was Maurice standing, in his cube, giving me very dirty looks, as if, he had a reason to be angry with me. I call this look his "stay away" look. He looked very intense with his fist up in the air as if he wanted to start a fight. I went back to my cube and waited until he was gone.

During all this time, I discovered that Maurice is capable of making all kinds of facial expressions to intimidate someone else. Such expressions as "I'm about to kill you" look or "Your Ass is so mine" type look.

After that first meeting, we took our usual walk in the park during our lunch hour, but as time passed, he came up with excuses of not going out with me (not feeling well, etc.). I began to walk alone in the park or with another friend at lunch.

He began going out to lunch with other members of our team and acted like he really didn't want anything to do with me.

The first month had passed, and Maurice had requested to talk to me for a second time. This time he was visibly angrier and had warned me not to talk about him behind his back. I again was on the defensive and explained to him that I didn't, nor would I ever do anything like that. He, of course, acted like he didn't believe me.

We ended up having these discussions for a total of three times, which took almost as many months. Our last discussion was, in his mind, was the very last straw (part of his act). Even though I always denied ever doing what he said or believed I did, it didn't matter. He acted like he was very angry with me. I mention "act" for a reason.

As far as I am concerned, everything he was doing was all an act to make me feel bad, and look bad in front of the others on the team. This also made it appear that I can't get along with others, which is a big no-no in any working environment.

Suddenly this man went from being my good friend to instantly being my absolute worst nightmare in a matter of minutes. He literally went from one extreme to the other. It was as if he pulled a 360 on me. He suddenly began making all sorts of false accusations about the quality of my work to my managers and others of my team. He was constantly saying negative things about me, both in front of me and behind my back. Then he did something else I didn't expect.

He called HR and began asking questions relating to how HR deals with ethics issues. He had made accusations about me and what I had supposedly done. Getting HR documents delivered to him via interoffice mail and displaying what he was looking at every time I went past his cube. When he was out of his cube, I stopped by to see that he was reviewing HR documentation on ethics issues.

He made several phone calls to HR (Human Resources) and made it a point to speak loud enough so that I could hear what he was talking about. He sounded as if I was a real problem and had to be dealt with. He was bullying me at the absolute worst degree. It was all mental abuse. The following are examples of what he was doing to me and is also mentioned as examples of workplace bullying.

It is literally as if he was using an anti-bully book and actually using it against me. When I began reading the book "The Bully at Work" I read the following as examples as to what bullying in the office. To make matters worse, I was actually experiencing what I was reading.

- Spreading malicious rumors
- Excluding or isolating someone socially
- Staring, dirty looks or other negative eye contacts
- Giving others the silent treatment
- Intentionally damning with faint praise
- Undermining or deliberately impeding someone's work
- Blaming someone for breakages or mistakes they didn't do
- Withholding important information or purposefully providing misinformation
- Verbally abusing, or making fun of you or your work (including your family, sexuality, race or culture, education or economic background, clothing, and accent)
- Creating a feeling of uselessness
- Persistently criticizing
- Belittling my opinions
- Invading someone's privacy by pestering, stalking or spying
- Tampering with someone's personal belongings or work equipment

He put on an act that he was so angry at me that he wanted to start a fight right there in the office. Rick, Jon, Chris, Eric, and others on the team had tried desperately to get him to stop, but he refused. Chris even told him that "no one wants a bully on the team." But that didn't stop Maurice. He just continued down this path of ruining whatever reputation I had in that department.

I even heard my boss, Eric, tell him to stop or he's fired, but that still didn't stop him. He continued until everyone on the team was worn out. Jon even explained to him that you don't treat another human being this way. But he just would not listen to anyone.

Eric wanted things to get back to the way things were when we were friends, but that could never happen. At this point, he had shown respect to everyone in the office except me.

With everyone on the team against him, he would not listen, and he kept continuing with this constant barrage of vicious harassment towards me.

There seemed to be nothing I could do. He continued down this path of non- stop harassment regardless as to what anyone said to him, including my Boss, Eric or any of the other managers.

While walking past his cube, I heard him telling my Boss that he has a mental illness specifically about me. He had told everyone that he had a real problem with me.

At this point, I was very numb and just didn't know or understand as to why he was doing this to me. As I mentioned before, I completely forgot what he had originally told me in the park on that fateful day.

This behavior was just the beginning. Stepping back from what was happening to me, I realized that all those walks with him during lunch was really just his way of getting me relaxed enough to discuss my personal life with him. My personal home life at that time was very complicated with the possibility of a divorce looming over my head as well as some other financial and family problems. But with all that, I believe that he had realized that my real fear was losing my position at Data Systems. Moving to EOD department was not my decision, and he knew that.

He knew this and did things, such as always coming into my space, which had made me very uncomfortable, and increased my fears and put me on edge.

He went down the path of pushing my buttons every chance he got. Whenever I was alone, he would put on an act like he tried to have a fist fight with me, both inside and outside the office.

He also once said that the time eventually would come when we would have a Death Match in the park. Idle threats such as this is just another example of what he had said to give me feelings of fear, along with all the other feelings I had been having.

When we were friends, I once told him that I once took the Chinese martial arts before I got married, and he said that he and his Daughter are both 3rd Degree black belts in the Korean martial art Tai Kwan Do. I now realize that by just pointing out that's he's a third degree was just another way to keep in control of me so that he could frighten me when he felt the need to.

I was very numb and was very nervous about what was going on. During the height of this bullying, he would sneak into my cube at times and make a scuffle, making it sound as if we are both fighting. The Senior Architect, Jon, would run over and tell him to stop it and then tell me just to ignore him.

There was actually one time when I was just standing there feeling numb. Jon was telling me to ignore him in one ear while at the same time the bully, Maurice was telling me that "I'm a stupid Shit" in the other. He was acting out this horrendous stuff while I was trying to perform well with me current job as a Sr. Developer.

All this had my head spinning, and at this point I was beginning to experience some mental illness symptoms.

I knew that I was being "bullied" so I had searched for someone who had actually specialized with PTSD patients (Post Traumatic Stress Disorder).

I was diagnosed with this condition from my new therapist in October 2005. I couldn't believe what my psychiatrist had told me. That I was beginning to have the same type of disorder that someone gets after being in a war zone.

As I mentioned earlier, others on the team had told Maurice that "no one likes a bully on the team" but he just wouldn't listen. He just kept up with all this severe bullying and developed the reputation that he just would not stop.

To keep my sanity, I began reading several books on the subject, including "The Bully at Work." This is an excellent book on the subject and is written by a Husband-and-Wife Psychology team Doctor's Gary and Ruth Namie, both PHD's.

There was one time when I actually called them. I asked them if there was anything I could do. In other countries such as the United Kingdom, I could have filed charges where the government would charge the perpetrator with bullying and pose stiff fines and penalties on them and then give the victim most of the money.

In this country, and especially during this period, I couldn't sue somebody just because he's a jerk. I heard that from two lawyers and the authors who wrote "The Bully at Work" book. I could have tried to sue him, but there's a good chance that I would have lost the case.

This bully also began doing something else which surprised everyone. He publicly began inviting everyone, except me to different functions, such as golf outings, lunches, etc. He made sure that I was present each time he did this.

What he was really doing was distancing me from the rest of the group. I was treated more and more like an outsider. As time went by, he was bullying me at one level, while at the same time, bullying everyone else in the group at different levels. This behavior continued day in and day out.

One time I was in the coffee room with another manager, making myself some coffee, when suddenly Maurice came over and asked that manager, who was standing next to me, if he wanted to participate in some real estate investment venture with him and several other members of the team. This Manager asked, "what about Bob?" Maurice said no and walked away. This type of behavior continued along with all his other bullying. The manager then asked me if I was OK. I turned and just looked at him. I wasn't OK; I was experiencing the PTSD condition my psychiatrist had told me about.

Later that day, everyone went down to the cafeteria for a corporate meeting. We sat down with all the other head managers. I was sitting in a middle row, and Maurice was sitting down two seats away from me. At this point, his mere presence had made me very uncomfortable.

I noticed our Senior VP, Harley, talking with Kevin. Harley asked him about Maurice. Kevin told him, "Oh, he's a real bully. He's just a bully." The Senior VP took a look at him, then took a look at me and just laughed.

Kevin actually appeared to be the only person to be on my side. That was great because he was a Director. But to everyone's surprise, the next morning, Kevin no longer worked with the company. No one ever found out as to why. He was just gone the next morning.

Another time I found a wedding Invitation on my desk. I couldn't believe that it actually came from Maurice. I stopped by his cube and congratulated him. He turned to me and said that he only invited me because he had to. I took that to mean that, with another disgusting look, that I wasn't actually invited.

The Monday after the wedding, he e-mailed everyone on the team a link to his wedding photos to everyone, including me. These were pictures of many members from the team who was there, including my manager, Eric, and his wife.

To me, it actually appeared that this wedding was merely another disassociating tool rather than an actual marriage out of love. He made it a point to use any activity, including this special event as a mere tool to disassociate me from the rest of the group.

He basically kept track of me at all times. Whether I was getting coffee, going to a meeting, going to lunch, going to the Men's room, he always seemed to know where I was at all times. It was as if this was his main job there at Data Systems because I didn't really see him doing much of anything else.

There was one time when I walked out of the men's room, went towards my cube when I noticed all the other members of the team just standing there with their coats on and holding their heads down.

The bully was standing alone over to the right side, next to where I had to go to get to my cube, looking at them. He then said; "you're ready?" And then he led the way where they all took off and went out to lunch together. I was clearly not invited.

This again was just another way to make me feel very uncomfortable with my job by disassociating me from the rest of the team.

I went to my boss several times. I pleaded with him to make him stop. That there was nothing, I did to him at all. At this point, he actually seemed to be siding with the bully. Many of the things that were done to me were done in public and were clearly done in front of the other managers. They basically just shook their heads and laughed with disbelief.

What was I supposed to do? Try to fight him in the office? I would have been immediately fired. Maurice made it quite clear to me that there was no talking to him. My immediate Boss was in total denial, and whenever he bullied me, my boss, Eric, and his lead Architect, Jon, would just slip it under the rug. They tried to keep the issue within our department, so everything that he did was covered up.

Then, one day, my Boss had told me that their HR representative would be flying in from Havertown PA to talk to the two of us and bring in any witnesses that he thought was necessary. This is the first time that my boss actually appeared to be on my side. I wish I still had that HR person's name because I could really use his insight while writing these pages.

On the morning of his arrival, I was nervous, but at the same time, I wish this would finally bring an end to all this bullying once and for all.

He first spoke to me, and then he spoke to Maurice. And finally, he brought me in to join in discussion with Maurice. Eric was present throughout all those meetings.

The first words out of Maurice's mouth were that he was having some personal issues at home and that he had told Eric that he was considering suicide. This surprised us all, but I then realized that this was a ploy so that HR will be very careful as to how to deal with him.

Others who sat in the general area were brought in for questioning, but I don't know what was actually discussed. I actually witnessed one time when Maurice was discussing these meetings with one of those witnesses telling her exactly what to say. She was arguing with him, and he was working with some of his bullying skills in an effort to change her story. I was still numb and confused during that time, so I didn't say anything to anybody.

Then later in the day, cameras were installed next to the bully's cube and in the surrounding areas. On the next day, the bullying started up again. There was even a time when I noticed the HR person talking to my manager about the very aggressive bullying he was seeing for himself.

Eric responded with "let's just wait and see." This talk was in the lunchroom as he was finishing up his meal with several of the other managers.

Basically, every time Maurice harassed me, all the witnesses seemed to pretend that they didn't see anything and the managers slipped it under the rug. I had the impression that they brought in that HR person to cover their own ass and nothing more.

House Warming Party - Invite from a friend

One day everyone in our team was invited over to one of our team mate's new home for a little house warming party. She was one of the new members of our team and had made it a point to make sure that I knew that I was invited.

So, we all went out during our lunch break. I went in my boss's van with part of the team and Maurice made it a point to go over in the other car with the rest of the folks. Everyone was aware of the situation between the two of us.

Mai was very friendly towards me and didn't take any of Maurice's BS. In fact, there were a couple of times when she did what you're supposed to do when there is a bully in the group. She stood up to him when no-one else would. Myself with me introverted personality and with the PTSD symptoms I was in a state of fear and shock to the point where I just couldn't muster up enough courage. I was numb and was afraid of what he might do if I did.

My Boss went into the kitchen to prepare some food, and Maurice just gave me one of his dirty looks and walked into the kitchen with him. He kept his back towards me and acted like he was discussing something with him. They were discussing something quietly where I couldn't hear what they were saying, but I didn't care. I just focused on making the best of the situation.

Maurice's negative energy filled the room during the whole event. His bullying is unbelievable. He has a real talent of generating very negative energy towards his victim. I was very nervous and upset.

Our hostess knew what was going on, so she came over and began talking with me. This helped me take my mind off of Maurice and his BS. We had a great conversation, and some of the others came over and acted friendly towards me and joining in our conversation. So eventually, I felt much more relaxed and ended up having a great time.

As we left to go back to the office, I noticed my boss sitting in his van watching Maurice and I, as we walked out of the house. Maurice took the lead, walking alone with all that negative energy. I was very uncomfortable. The following picture doesn't show it, but there was a nice archery set leaning against the side of the house.

I was walking with the others, but I stopped for a moment staring at that set. I wondered for a moment what would have happened if I picked it up and pointed an arrow at Maurice. He suddenly turned around, giving me one of his evil stares while continually walking backwards. Some of the others quietly told me just to keep ignoring him and just to don't pay him any mind. Except for our hostess, this was the first time that most of my teammates seemed supportive of me instead of the bully. I think that they simply felt sorry for me.

After we got back to the office, I made it a point to thank that nice woman for the invitation. She asked me if I tried talking to Maurice. I said I tried several times, and he made it absolutely clear to me that he did not ever want to talk to me again. I told her that I just don't know what to do with this constant barrage of BS. I was having a lot of problems dealing with all this.

She had to get back to work, and I went back to my cube to make an effort to get some of my work done.

Following me home after work

One bright sunny day after work is a day I will never forget. My trip home from Delaware to Pennsylvania was usually an hour and a half if you include the daily traffic jams on I-95 and the Blue route which connects to the Pennsylvania Turnpike. The distance I had to travel on Interstate 95 was just thirteen miles.

One day, while I was stuck on I-95, I noticed a black Mercedes jerk suddenly, as if to miss hitting my car. I then turned around and realized that it was actually Maurice. He just sat there with a very horrific stare at me as if he was about to attack me. This is the same type of stare I once witnessed Arash doing during that time in the traffic jam when we once worked together.

Maurice's ability to give such a horrifying stare is what he does as part of the bullying of his victims. I felt shocked, a sense of fear, and didn't really know what to do. He acted like he was going to ram my car or worse yet get out of his car and assault me. His actions were so frightening that I didn't stop to think to dial 911 or anything on my cell phone. I just wanted to get out of the traffic jam and get the hell home.

When I finally arrived at the entrance to the Blue Route, I noticed that he had pulled his car off to the side of the road as I turned right onto the entrance, while continuing with his horrible angry stares.

The next morning, I made it a point to tell everyone in the office what he had done. No one, including Eric, had said anything. They just looked at me with utter disbelief.

With such poor responses from my teammates, I felt very depressed and discouraged. This bully was building the reputation that he would do the types of things, of which was very hard to believe by anyone. Who in their right mind could ever do such things to another human being?

My reaction was to try to let all this crap roll off my shoulders, and to try not to let all this interfere with my work performance. That was really hard. To this day, I am amazed by the fact that I was actually still able to get the work done on or ahead of schedule.

That said, I also realized that my days at this company were numbered. I was on the way out, and everyone knew it. And there was absolutely nothing that I could do.

Golf Outing - 2005

There was a Golf outing that my friend Andrew, one of the Senior Analysts from a different department, had organized and made sure that I would be allowed to participate in. It was twilight golf where we left early that day and played as many holes as possible before it got dark. Andrew knew Maurice's bullying tactics and what he was really up to.

On the day of the golf outing, several of the other teammates were in Maurice's cube, trying to talk him into going with rest of us on the outing. He told everyone that he would be there, but he wasn't going with us in our group.

He was going with someone else to the same course on that day. That the only way, we would be able to recognize him was with him wearing a red t- shirt and a fatigue hat.

When we got to the course, we went into the pro-shop to check in and schedule our time on the course.

After we teed off the first hole, we started to find each other's balls. After we approached the first green, someone else behind us was shooting balls while we were still on the green.

Usually, each group waits until after the group ahead of him leaves so that no one will get hurt. But this person acted like he was trying to hit us. Luckily that didn't happen. This activity had continued until after we were finishing up on the last hole.

But on the last green, something else happened. While finishing up our last green, I noticed across from us a man with a red t-shirt and light-colored fatigue hat staring at me as if he was going to kill me. He just continued this stair directly at me, while his companion was continually driving his golf cart around in circles.

The man in the cart finally stopped and asked Maurice what the hell he was doing. He supposedly talked one of his karate buddies to go with him on this trip. The man in the cart realized that he made a big mistake and told Maurice that he was wrong and that he was leaving.

This whole scene demonstrates just how this bully can talk people into going along with him.

The next day, I overheard Maurice described that his partner was a 6th- degree black belt and that he kept driving the golf cart in circles so that I wouldn't be able to identify him. Maurice was just non-stop with all this kind of harassment.

I remember another time when we all went out to another Golf Outing. To everyone's surprise, Maurice went along. During the play, I would hit the ball after Maurice.

Maurice went ahead of us when we were hitting onto the green. He then would go and deliberately begin playing with my ball. This was just another excuse to bully me and see if I would react.

The Other Woman

One of the women who worked on the Tandem side of our system called me out of the clear blue and invited me out to lunch. I'll name her Mary. She was a stunningly beautiful woman but was partially disabled with a bad knee.

She walked with a cane, so I drove my car over to pick her up at the front door. She got in, and we went off to the nearby Olive Garden restaurant around the corner from our office.

She was very nice, and I must admit I was somewhat surprised by her interest in me. But anyway, we finished our meal and headed back to the office.

When we got back to the front door, she did something which really surprised me. She places her hand cupped in front of my groin as if she wanted to grab me and go to town.

I just looked at her, and she continued staring at me with such a lovely smile. WOW, the temptation was there, but with being married, I wasn't quite ready to go astray.

I told her that I had to go to the office, so we parted ways. We planned to go out again sometime.

The very next morning while walking to my cube, I overheard the bully talking to some of his friends, describing Mary and saying that if you buy her lunch, she will give you a blow job. He invited his friends to go with him.

Again, just another form of bullying where he had to go out to lunch with someone I went out with. This is totally unbelievable, just another excuse to harass me.

After I went back upstairs after my lunch, I looked out my office window where could I see them getting out of the car. I could see

Mary fondling Maurice's friend sitting in the back seat and Maurice standing outside to the right of the car, staring up at me with this huge grin on his face.

What an ass, if it's not one thing with this bully, it's something else to drive me over the edge.

Mary wasn't the only woman in the office who was very sexually active. There were others in my area that ran a sex club where they met at a nearby motel and had orgies.

One day, the woman running the group had actually stopped by my cube and Maurice's cube and invited us to join in on the fun. I couldn't believe it. I turned and just looked at her and said absolutely not. I then went back to what I was doing.

Maurice even came over and asked if I wanted to go. I just looked at him and told him to go away, which he did.

Temporary Insanity

By this time, all this horrific and very aggressive style of bullying had come to a head, and I just couldn't take it anymore. I was constantly harassed both in public and privately by this guy. I was made to feel that I just wasn't worth anything. I remember another time when I was alone in the parking lot, walking to my car, when Maurice snuck up behind me, slammed me up against my car and said "Why are you still here? You're not welcome here. You need to leave".

Then he walked away. I was mortified with all this violent behavior. The next morning, I told my boss. Eric walks into his cube and point blank asks Maurice if he assaulted me in the parking lot last night. He replied, "I didn't do that…" My boss then walked away and went back to his office.

Besides running into my cube and making sounds as if we are both fighting, he would also throw fake punches at me trying to get me to flinch. He also was continually coming into my space to the point where I was always nervous and put on edge.

When I was asked to work with him on a project, and I went into his cube, he would suddenly scream and holler as if I was hurting him. He constantly would tell my boss and others all kinds of lies and BS.

All this crap was continuing while I was required to get my work done on schedule. At this point, it was as if Maurice's primary function was to harass me as much as possible with the hopes that I would eventually resign.

Temporary Leave of Absence from the Office

During all this time, undergoing all this absurd bullying, I began to show signs of being physically sick. It's 2006, and my regional enteritis (a form of Crone's Disease – inflammation of the small intestines) came out of remission and began acting up with some abdominal pain and nausea. I was experiencing borderline peritonitis and was being scheduled for emergency surgery at the Lansdale Hospital for my second Bowel Resection surgery.

I must admit I was nervous about the surgery because of just how serious the operation really is. But at the same time, I was glad to be out of the office for a while. I remember there were times when I felt relieved when Maurice took a sick day. Amazingly, life was great without that bully around.

When I went into the hospital in August 2006, I was first scheduled to be out of the office for about six weeks. Then, shortly after I was released from the hospital, I had a muscle seizure, and after a visit to a neurologist, I had my license suspended for an additional six months.

My boss wasn't happy about this but what choice did he have. I ended up working from home on light duty for a while. With no more seizures within the six months, I was granted my license back and was on my way back to the office.

One time I actually remembered Eric calling for me and my Wife answered the phone. She told him that I wasn't available and then she asked him about Maurice. My boss was in a state of total denial. He acted like there wasn't any real problem with him at all.

Back in the Office

I finally returned to work with a clean bill of health from my doctors in May 2007. That day the whole team, including myself and Maurice, went out to lunch together.

Maurice, to my surprise, had made it a point to ride in the same car that I was in. On the way to the restaurant, Maurice, who was sitting in the passenger seat in front of me, had asked me how I was feeling. He asked if it was safe for me to work under stress. With the way he was asking me these questions, I had the distinct impression that what he really wanted was to know if it was safe enough for him to begin with his bullying again. Everyone else in the car seemed stunned, and I didn't dare say a word.

Shortly after we returned, the VP of our department had called me down to his office for a talk (my bosses, boss). Calling me directly was very unusual. I thought that, for some reason, they might be planning on firing me. And when I went to the office and the HR woman showed up, I really thought I was about to be history.

Then they both calmed me down and told me that they were considering the possibility of outsourcing my position to India. If they decided to move forward with this idea, and if I had accepted their offer, that I would receive a 10% bonus plus six month's severances. They also said that this would be their best and final offer they could give me.

I was thinking: "So I'm not being fired today, but it looks like my days are definitely numbered. Yeah right, after ten hard years this is the best offer, they could do?" I felt that I really didn't have a choice but to take their offer. It would also be a way to finally get Maurice's BS out of my life for good.

At this time Maurice had his bullying back in full swing. I felt that if he hadn't, I might have actually asked for a better offer. The managers in our area were fully aware as to what Maurice was doing to me and did nothing to stop it. Oh, my boss did tell him to back off, but he just wouldn't stop. It seemed that the more Eric told him to stop, the more bullying he did. It was just never-ending.

I remember one time when the Lead Architect of our department, Jon, had told my boss that Maurice was going to HR about this whole thing. What did my boss say? "Bob is merely a casualty of the situation and must leave the company."

Anything that Maurice threw at me, they just kept slipping under the rug. As I mentioned earlier, I read some books on the subject and sought some professional help and were eventually diagnosed with Post Traumatic Stress Disorder.

June 1st came, and I was called into the VP office for the second time. He told me that they had decided to go forward with outsourcing my position to India. He suggested that I have the documents checked by an attorney and to have them signed and submitted within 48 hours. I did just that, and he told me that an on sight and offshore persons from India would be in later this week. From this point forward, for the next 60 days, I would be working directly with him (the VP) and that my primary responsibility will be to train these two people my job.

When they arrived, I realized that both of them could hardly speak a word of English. This would be a real challenge for me, but I realized that I had to do my best. My last day was August 31st 2007.

With everything that was involved, I wrote a lot of documentation and, especially to get away from the bully, I held several meetings in conference rooms. The rest of the team basically left me alone.

Maurice continued with his harassment whenever we were not in the meetings. One time after the rest of the team found out about my situation, Maurice went around acting upset stating that he was on the list to be outsourced as well.

For a moment, I actually felt good. Then our manager and Senior Architect went in his cube and asked him as to where the hell did, he get that idea? He was not on any list. What did Maurice say in front of the whole team, including me? "Well, at least I still got a Job." Just another harassment statement designed to make me feel alone, depressed with very low self- esteem.

The outsourcing continued through these 60 days and Maurice's BS bullying continued, whenever I wasn't in any meeting. When I was in meetings, he had made it a point to give me one of his dirty looks through the window of the door. Since the managers had allowed it, I distinctly had the impression that they wanted this added pressure on me in the hopes that I would just give up and quit, where I wouldn't be entitled to their offers.

I remember that I had made one big mistake where I ended up on the wrong side of the Senior VP, Harley. He was in charge of all our systems during that time. To this day I'm not sure as to why he had an issue with me other than the fact that, in the beginning, when we were designing and developing all this software, I showed some low self-confidence in myself and my work.

I had enough smarts to make everything work but didn't have the type of personality he preferred to have in any of his departments. As far as I could see, those that excelled in that company are the bafflers and bullies. It's the type of environment where no one should ever have to work in.

I think they were surprised by the fact that I put in 100% effort with the outsourcing that had lasted the full 60 days. What was driving me was not the fact that I would receive that bonus and severance. It was the fact that I would finally be away from Maurice. I wouldn't have to worry about him anymore. I could finally relax and go on with the rest of my life.

Now, looking back with all that has happened to me, I realize just how wrong that last sentence is. If Maurice hadn't followed me around the country where I was working, as he did, that I might not have even written this book.

I believe that he has a real ego issue where he feels that since he got away with his harassment towards me in one company, that he would be able to get away with his harassment towards me again and again. I wouldn't be surprised if he's still keeping tabs on me even though I'm listed as retired.

Leaving Data Systems Corporation – *Position Outsourced to India*

Well, it's finally August 31st 2007, and it's my last day in the office. I must admit that I was choked up a bit, mainly because I spent over ten years of my life in this place, and it had finally come to an end. The only good thing was that I was finally away from that bully who had made my life a living hell. At least so I thought.

He had selected me and used me as a means to an end. I said it while this was all going on and I will repeat it. This poor excuse for a human being had lied to everyone, management, HR, and all the employees in the area where we had worked.

I went around the office and said my goodbyes to all my friends. Even my managers who basically were glad to see me leaving. The manager of Card Management Department came over and felt sorry for me, so she gave me a big hug. I was in tears, and she felt sorry it all happened this way.

One of the senior managers actually had the gall to imply that I was making some kind of sexual advances toward her, where they could have fired me on the spot and where I would also have lost my severance and bonus. She immediately told him to "stow it", or she would go directly to HR and report him if he didn't stop. "He's been through enough", she said.

TARGETED

I went out the door never to return again. I drove my final hour and fifteen minutes home and sat outside my back porch.

- CHAPTER THREE -

After Data Systems

It was a great feeling that I was finally away from that horrible bully. With all the harassment that I was faced with at Data Systems daily, I must admit that I had many fantasies of getting even. I have been having a lot of thoughts of throwing in the towel and going postal. My therapist, who had been treating me with the PTSD, had told me on several occasions that these feelings are actually normal.

I know the managers and other staff members of my old team were either covering up what the bully did to me or tried to ignore him whenever possible.

Imagine, if I did walk into the office with a gun and shot my boss, the bully, and several of the other members of the team, and to top it off with my bosses after I did all that I most likely would have taken my own life.

When I had these feelings, I talked to my therapist about them but also kept thinking of my adorable grandson. During that very dark period of my life, my grandson and I were very close. When I looked into his eyes, I know in my heart that I could never do anything that could ever jeopardize my being prevented from ever seeing him again, especially through his years of growing up.

Every time I hear of someone going on a rampage in either a school or in some office, I believe that bullying had something to do with it somewhere along the perpetrator's life.

After I relaxed for a week, I began to look for ways to improve my technical skills. I went online and found Polaris Learning Solutions, which is owned and operated by someone who has a sound knowledge of Tandem computer systems.

The owner/instructor, Scott and I became great friends over the years, and I bought into their Tandem online TACL course. I learned a lot and later was able to use him as a mentor from time to time as he helped me with getting up to speed on the Tandem Systems and some of that technology which I felt that I would need in my profession.

The best thing was that I was finally away from that horrible bully. I continued with the psychotherapy, which helped me deal with my PTSD and helped me deal with all the anger I had with Data Systems Corporation and that horrible bully, Maurice.

Even though I was away from him, I had many sleepless nights. PTSD is a complicated mental illness to deal with. I know my personality had suffered from this, especially since I was planning to go on the road as a consultant. To this day, I always have dark feelings about what happened to me, and I still look over my shoulder to see if Maurice is in the area.

After leaving the Data Systems office for the last time, I relaxed for a few months, focused on bringing myself up to speed, and by December 2007, I began searching for a new contract. I was able to afford my COBRA medical expenses, mortgage, and our other household expenses from the severance I was on. I found and was accepted on my first contract in Austin, TX.

That contract only lasted a total of six weeks because I really wasn't up to speed with the type of programming they were doing. The good news was that I actually got some experience as a contractor. I came home and then was offered another contract in Eden Prairie, MN.

This contract only lasted two months. The company had its share of dirty politics, and I got in the middle of it all, so another contract had come to an end. I realized that there are many companies of all sizes which all seem to have their share of bullies.

I left that company, and my cell phone basically rang off the hook. After several Phone interviews, I finally was accepted for a new position in Little Rock, Arkansas.

I packed my bags from Minneapolis and drove down to Little Rock AR. When I arrived, I wondered if I actually had the job. I spent several weeks at a nearby hotel while I waited for them to get all the necessary paperwork in order. I checked with my head hunter, and she assured me that I would begin working shortly.

My Friend Rick – after we are both out of Data Systems

Rick, a friend of mine from my old department at Data Systems, was laid off around six months after I had left. We kept in touch over the years, supporting each other as we went to work at other companies. Rick feels that he's a friend of mine and also a friend of Maurice's.

Whenever we talked, he had always made it a point to explain to me that he had created multiple web pages on the social networks (Facebook, LinkedIn) and that I saw one version (web page) and Maurice saw another. Maurice always knows how to get others to stand behind him, and Rick was just another example.

I tried several times to convince him what Maurice was and what he was really doing, but it seemed to go on deaf ears.

I explained what Maurice had originally told me that one day, several years ago, in the park, and no matter what I said, he just didn't believe me. My story was just so unbelievable. Who would ever consider on spending all this time and effort on little old me? Why was I so important?

The only thing I knew was the fact that I was responsible for a very high profile, piece of a very complex system. Eric had me teach this guy my system as a backup, and as soon as he knew it, he decided to bully me to the extent where I would just quit under disgust.

Then once I was out of the way, he would take over my system and discuss how he could make all sorts of changes to increase optimization etc. With his talent of getting others on the team to do things for him, I'm sure that he would be very successful in doing just that.

What choice would my old boss have? No one else on the team knew the programs as well as he did.

Rick, my boss, and others on the team were just examples of how this horrific bully spread his reign of terror throughout Data Systems. There was no reasoning with Maurice. He made it appear that I was the person they had to get rid of.

I was made to look like I was the bad guy, no matter what I said. While I was out on sick leave with my surgery, my managers grew to believe this. They didn't care what supposedly happened between us or what I supposedly did. As far as I was concerned, Maurice had made the whole thing up. That there was absolutely nothing, I had ever done to him.

After I left, Rick would call me from time to time, letting me know how things were after I had left and about Maurice. Maurice always talked about me and the code I worked on. Maurice had also mentioned to everyone where I was working.

I was able to learn that Maurice was always able to keep tabs of me as he was able to crack jokes about me and where I was. Rick had told me that he was very funny.

Whatever reputation I had there was totally gone. I would never be able to work there again. He made sure of that by continually bad mouthing me every chance he got. Departments and people had changed over the years, but one thing still remains. Maurice, the worst bully I had ever met, is still working there. Last I heard, he's working on some on-call support department and is not really doing any more programming.

Visit's in Little Rock

When I finally began working in Little Rock AR, I soon realized that I worked right down the street from President Clinton's Library, the office of one of the Arkansas Senators was around the corner of where we work, and out back of our office was where many famous singers put on a show when they came to town. I saw BB King, Willy Nelson, ZE ZE Top, to mention just a few.

I also didn't know what Southern Hospitality really meant until after I resided there and had experienced that firsthand. Most people, especially after they get to know you, show a lot of love and treat you like your part of their family. It was a wonderful experience.

My contract lasted for six months and was later extended for another two months. I worked hard and was having a great time. By the end of the eight months, I was made an offer to work full time. The manager there made me a very low offer, but since I was desperate, I took the position anyway.

I know now that I had made a big mistake there because I had completed my first successful contract since Data Systems. I should have continued with the contracting where I would have continued to make a lot more money.

I was down here for about two and a half years before I ran into my old adversary from Data Systems (that asshole bully who almost completely ruined my life and career). Remember that golf outing back in 2005? Here's what he did.

One day while leaving work for the day, I was walking down to the office parking lot to get to my car. A man had suddenly appeared right out of nowhere asking me for some money (begging panhandler).

I told him that the police down here had told us not to give out any handouts. I also suggested that he should leave before the police catch him. He just looked at me, and I actually thought that he looked very familiar.

After I walked down near my car, I looked back at that beggar and then I saw something I didn't expect. The man stood there staring at me with the much familiar fatigue hat.

This was really bizarre. He was actually here. He stared at me just like he did before, looking like he was about to go for me jugular. Then suddenly out of nowhere came a brown station wagon. The woman driver pulled up next to Maurice, where he leapt into the back seat and continued with his staring at me as I ran down the street towards their car as it drove off.

The next evening, after I went back to my apartment from the store, I stepped out for a minute to get the rest of the groceries out of my car. When I did that, I noticed an old white sedan positioned down ways where I had parked my car. Two people were in the car, and they appeared to be waiting for somebody in the complex.

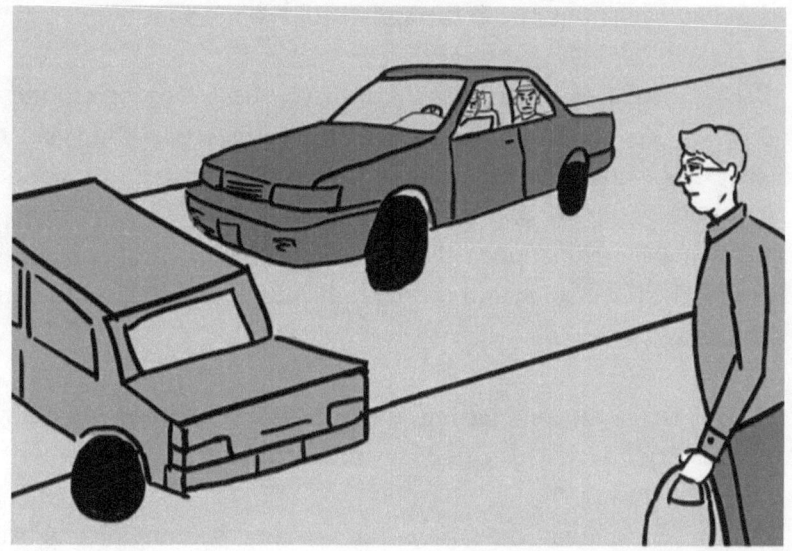

While putting away my order, I heard some commotion outside so I went outside to check. I saw the same white sedan and both guys outside the car. They appeared to be changing a flat tire. One of the men was staring at me while crouched down on the other side of the car. I thought nothing of it, so I went back into my apartment.

The next morning, after I began driving to work, I felt the wind on the passenger side. The windows on the passenger side were smashed, and there was glass everywhere. It appeared that someone had sabotaged my car in the apartment complex parking lot where I was living. The entire passenger side had been smashed in. It looked like it was hit by some utility truck (or so what I was told at the auto body shop).

I reported the incident to the police. Why didn't I report Maurice to the Little Rock Police who examined my car? I attribute that to what he did to me with all his horrific staring. All the frightening bullying he has done to me had really taken its toll, and while I was out of town, I wasn't being treated for PTSD.

When he does his bullying, I immediately shut down with a lot of fear, and I really don't want to acknowledge his presence. Also, I felt that no one would ever believe me. When I see this horrible person, a lot of horrible memories come to the surface. I felt I couldn't prove anything so I left him out of the story I told to the police.

When the car was being repaired, the rubber stripping around the window was also damaged. The mechanic at the repair shop had told me that the damage to the stripping was not related to the accident, so they were going to skip that specific repair. I explained that it was related, but they still skipped that part of the repair. To this day, I still hear the whistling of the wind on the right side of my 2002 Ford Taurus while driving.

I do have a distinct feeling that he had something to do with it. The history I have had with Maurice is unbelievable.

Whenever we are in the same room together, he immediately begins to act like he's going to attack me or start some sort of ruckus where I will be in some way involved.

Four years came and went, and I was in a big lay off with the company in Little Rock. Almost two months later, I landed my first new contract in Pittsburgh, PA. The main office where I will be working was in Pennsylvania.

Excited with my good fortune, I went and told the property manager at the Riverfront apartment complex where I was staying. And I also told all my good friends down there, and they all wished me luck.

I was able to live down there with the INETECH compensation payments I have been receiving. I then began packing up and actually mailing most of my stuff home.

TARGETED

On one bright sunny day, I stepped outside and noticed a party starting in the apartment above me and several people coming home from work.

Then suddenly I saw him. Maurice was taking a tour of our apartments. The woman property manager who I discussed my situation with was giving him the tour.

She pointed to me and told him my situation and that I was leaving at the end of September. He then took one look at her, then pointed and me and said "really?".

Then he suddenly began to leave and I started following him towards the office. He jumped in his car and took off, yelling that he will see me later. At that time, I didn't understand what he meant.

September 29, 2012, finally came, and I said my final goodbyes to Arkansas and began my drive home to PA.

My first day at my new position was scheduled for October 15, 2012. It was finally nice to be able to get home and be with my Wife and family for a short while before reporting for work only four hours away. This felt great, and my check would be almost double what I use to get from my previous job. I was in seventh heaven.

- CHAPTER FOUR -

New Contract in Pittsburgh PA

After over a five-hour drive from PA, I arrived at the Extended Stay America in Carnegie, PA on October 12th. I was very excited about my new position.

As I got out of my car and walked towards the entrance to the motel, I heard a commotion from a group of people over to my left.

I turned and looked. "Oh My God, that's him," said the person in the car. "That's really him".

Now I'm thinking: "Oh My God, Is that my worst nightmare, Maurice? What should I do?"

As I'm checking in at the front desk, I hear someone come in, and as she did, I hear Maurice say "Jonna, He is gone. He is so gone".

So, Maurice was there, and again I did what I normally did and tried to ignore him.

When I went into my new room, I heard someone else say: "He's in room 103".

It really amazes me just how Maurice is capable of getting other people to do things for him. He is a real master to pull the right strings to get others to help set the stage for his bullying plans. OMG and I'm being targeted again by the same creep who had begun his reign of terror on me back at Data Systems in 2005. I just don't know what to do.

Eventually, I moved to an apartment complex in Wexford, PA. My new boss really liked that idea.

On October 15th, I promptly made it to the main office in Pittsburgh to get my new Badge. After that, I drove over to the office, which is set in a beautiful modern complex with two other companies (Mermaid Appliances and a private research laboratory for another popular company). I met my new Boss, Charles, and began getting all set up so I could begin doing my work.

Meeting with my worst nightmare at a new job location

The following morning, as I turned up the drive, I noticed someone in a car parked at the entrance talking to someone on his cell phone.

As I approached the parking lot where I was to park in front of Building

#4, someone had motioned me to stop to allow pedestrians to cross over and go into the front door of building #4. That's when I first saw Maurice at this facility. He had slowly walked across the drive-in front of me. Three associates from the Mermaid Appliances office had stood across from both me and Maurice laughing their asses off.

After I parked my car and walked up towards them, Maurice had walked ahead of me with his friends, carrying a gym bag. When he signed in at the Mermaid Appliances Security desk, he made some remarks where everyone at the doorway, including the security guards, just stood there and laughed, while looking in my direction.

Again, I just looked stunned as I walked away. On that morning he was carrying a gym bag, so I figured that he was either there visiting a friend or was employed with Mermaid Appliances.

I saw Maurice in the office many times during the three months I was there.

Each time he walked into the office, he was escorted in with members from Mermaid Appliances, and he signed in at the Mermaid Appliances front Security desk. I then realized that he was interviewing with them. His friend he knew at Mermaid Appliances is the same person I recognized who once worked at Data Systems on the same floor as my old department.

I also realized that each time he saw me; he focused on defaming my character to the group, he was with and the Mermaid Appliances security guards. He had a reputation of doing that every chance he got, especially when I was in the same area, he's in.

When I first saw Maurice at my new job. I was stunned with disbelief. A lot of very bad memories had kicked in. October 16, 2012, was my second day at my new job as a Tandem Consultant for City Ward Financial.

I basically ignored him, with his horrific stares, thinking that my job was secure. I realize now that, that was a huge mistake.

I was meeting all the required work either on or ahead of schedule. My Boss even had told me that I was doing a great job. I was in seventh heaven. I honestly had no idea that with this horrible bully in my presence that my days were really numbered.

Work was very busy upstairs, and I was accomplishing everything I was asked to do. During the Thanksgiving and Christmas weeks, I made provisions with Charles to take extended weekends off over those two holidays, which allowed me to drive home to visit my family.

My new Boss, Charles, had told me that I'm doing a great job right before I left for the Christmas Holliday. Again, I was in seventh heaven.

He was also happy with the fact that I found a nearby apartment where I was only eight miles away from the office. Feeling secure in my new job, I joined the nearby Tang Soo Do Karate school where I met many friends. I thought I would at least last through October 2013 and hopefully get extended for a second year. Boy was I wrong.

Since Charles had told me that I was doing a great job, I felt that my position there was secure. I had no idea that my position would soon be terminated. I had no idea that this could ever happen to me. I felt secure at this time, and I was really on cloud nine.

Building Security

Then one time, I noticed one of the Mermaid Appliances security guards visiting the area where I was working. He gave me a very dirty look, then turned to Charles and told him that he needed to have a talk with him in private. They went into a conference room and talked for around a half hour. My Boss didn't say anything to me, but from the looks of that security guard, I had a definite feeling it was about me. I had ignored what was going on and just continued with doing my work.

Escorted out of the building by security

At the end of the day, Charles asked me if I could work later to get some work done. I agreed. He mentioned that he needed to leave early, so I was working alone on that night.

Then suddenly that same security guard, who spoke to my boss earlier, came over to my cube and told me that I had to leave.

He first said, "I know who you are" while giving me a dirty look. Long story short, I had to leave because I was only a consultant and not a full-time employee.

I explained to him that my boss said I could work later, but that didn't matter. In his eyes, he was in charge since my boss wasn't around anywhere. So, I was escorted out of the building.

I have to admit that Maurice has impeccable timing. The modern architectural design of the building we were in had windows everywhere. It was like working in a glass house. Anyway, the following are brief explanations of the types of bullying activities I was confronted with on almost a daily basis.

Interrupting a meeting with my new team members

One day while we were in a meeting on the first floor, Maurice was standing right outside our window in the smoking area. At first, his back is facing towards us. Next, he slowly turned around with one of his horrible stares directed towards me. Others in the meeting had also noticed this.

Our meeting suddenly came to a temporary halt with everyone in the room, having stunned looks on their faces.

I also heard his friends from Mermaid Appliances sitting over at the nearby picnic table laughing and making snarling comments.

TARGETED

This time, I absolutely couldn't just ignore him, as I did in the past. Maurice was right outside my window and the Manager who was interviewing Maurice in our neighboring company and Maurice's friend was right outside, sitting at a picnic table.

I got up and ran to the entrance of the smoking area, with my hands on the door, my boss ran after me, and as I began opening the door, he said: "Bob if you open that door, I'll have to terminate our contract."

I was all set to go out and speak to that manager about my history with Maurice.

I took one look at Maurice, who was just standing there smiling at me with another one of his stupid looks.

Since that day, I was about to witness several other incidents from that bully before I was discharged.

Escorted across building complex to another meeting

One time my boss was escorting me to the other end of the building to an important meeting. On the way, we passed a group of people who were escorting Maurice to an interview with the company I was with. As we walked by, Maurice began to shake his head and said: "I can't believe you guys actually hired this guy" (meaning me). My boss and I both heard that remark. Then he made another remark which made everyone laugh. My boss said, "do you know this guy?" I said I did, but as usual, I was in a state of disbelief and kept silent.

Visit from our senior director of HR

Another time I was leaving the lunch room and heading to the elevator to return back to my office. One day on the way back, I ran into my boss and another manager talking. I overheard that manager say "no one with such a poor reputation deserves to be up there making 50 an hour." Then he quieted down as he took one look at me.

As my boss and I went into the elevator, I asked him who he was. He told me that he was the Senior Director of HR. Charles also said that he might need to do something. I just looked at him. I again basically ignored the whole thing.

A Close Encounter

Another blow hit me during the week before New Year's. The area where I usually ate my lunch was closed off for vendors who were invited in to sell their goods. On that day I needed to eat my lunch at the main part of the cafeteria. While I was eating my lunch, Maurice had suddenly walked in while staring at me with one of his dirty looks.

He sat down in front of me with his back facing towards me while he sat down to eat his meal. Then suddenly he turned "Completely" around and kept staring at me for about another eight to ten minutes. He had one of his "your ass is so mine" type stares. He was staring at me while swinging his right arm from right to left.

While he was doing that, the security guard who once escorted me out of the building came into the room giving me dirty looks.

That also bothered me as well, so I ignored it as much as possible.

As usual I didn't acknowledge Maurice either and just continued with eating my lunch. With the history we had in the past at Data Systems, I felt that if I acknowledged any of his constant staring's, that he would make some kind of scene and that I might have been immediately dismissed. As I mentioned before, I was just a contractor, not an employee.

I saw several people in the lunchroom observing what was going on. To this day, I don't know what kind of horrible lies he had been telling people, but they must have been real beauties.

After I finally finished my meal, I got up and left. As I did, I stopped a bit and looked at the bully while he was cussing to himself ("Oh Shit").

I actually sat down for a minute across from him. He started mumbling to me "I'm, I'm sorry", and then he sat back in his chair and calmly stared at me.

I asked: "Maurice, what did you do?" I just looked at him while in a state of shock. I know he spread lies to those I was working with, and I just didn't know what to do.

Bully's final day in building

On the beginning of what was to be my final week there, I saw Maurice being escorted out of the building for the last time. I distinctly remember the Dialogue between the bully, the manager who was interviewing him at Mermaid Appliances, and his friend who was with them whenever he was being escorted in and out of the building.

Maurice: Mumbling something as he's walking out of the building.

Manager: "Friday is his last day"

Maurice: "When do you want me to start?"

Manager: "I'll have to get back to you on that..."

Maurice: Yelling, "WHAT DO YOU MEAN, YOU TOLD ME THAT I HAD THE JOB."

Manager: "We thank you, I guess for alerting us about him. I wonder if you even know what you did. If you weren't here, he would still be working here. The truth is that you're a big bully and I let you go because I just wanted to see what you're capable of. You could have done this to any of my other staff members."

"I don't want you anywhere near the other members of my team. You just might be the worst bully I have ever seen."

Maurice's Friend: "You're a big bully Maurice, you're a big bully."

Manager: "Since you're not an employee, you are no longer allowed to use our gym."

Maurice's Friend: "You're a big bully Maurice, you're a big bully."

Maurice: "I guess you were just testing me."

Manager: "Yes".

Maurice: "OK". And then he turned to me and grinned directly at me as if to say "well I successfully got you fired", then he turned around and walked to his car...

The other two walked towards me while I was waiting for the elevator.

The three of us then walked into the elevator. On the way up, I asked them if that was Maurice.

They both said yes.

Then they got off on the third floor, to their office, and the manager was angry with Maurice's friend, asking him if he knew that he was going to do this?

He hemmed and hawed, and assured him that I wouldn't take any legal action.

I found out the hard way, what happens when you don't properly document this type of behavior. It was as if a horrible plague had swept through that building. He evidently had said things where it didn't really matter how good of a job I was doing. They just had to get rid of me. It was as simple as that.

On the following Friday, I received a surprise e-mail from the consulting firm that I was employed with. It said to call them right away. I called them, and the head hunter said that today was my last day. I was totally stunned and in complete shock! I just couldn't believe it. Oh My God! That Bastard got me fired. What the hell could I have done?

Evidently, he will never stop with his constant bullying attitude towards me. To my sudden surprise, I was let go. Charles said that he wasn't happy with my style of coding. With all the coding I did with getting the two batch refresh jobs working correctly and all the other work I did, and above all, meeting all the deadlines, I just couldn't understand if this was the only reason. We had code reviews of my work and everything looked fine. What did I suddenly do wrong?

He was concerned that I put my "and" and "or" statements over to the right instead of the left. I made all the appropriate changes but that still weren't good enough. He felt that I couldn't get up to speed fast enough. So, I suddenly was let go after 94 days – January 25, 2013. I later found out that I was let go due to poor performance (What HR had reported to the consulting firm I worked for).

The real reason why I was fired is from all that BS that Maurice said to everyone about me. Maurice had defamed my character to the point of ridiculous. And people just believed him and no one, and I mean no one said anything to me.

Charles's reasons were very poor excuses for me being dismissed. Maurice is very believable to those he has come in contact with. He had been talking to the Security Guards from the building entrance, and to several members of my staff about me, defaming my character left and right. I'm certain that some if not all of that information had made its way up to my boss, via that one security guard, as well as that Senior HR director, who both gave me dirty looks whenever they saw me. And this is NO exaggeration, and I am NOT paranoid. This really happened.

That bully says things very convincingly to those he feels can determine what my future will be. I feel that I will always have problems with this horrible bully wherever I go to and at any new job location. I feel that my only option is to go public with my story finally. I just don't know what else to do to fix this.

If I tried to sue him, there is a good chance that I would lose. At least that's what an employment attorney had told me. It's very difficult to sue someone for bullying. Taking photographs in these companies are strictly forbidden.

If I pulled out my phone camera and took a picture of him, he would have noticed it and would most likely have made a scene.

That said, the next time I'm working on a new job, and I run into him again, I'm going to disregard any rule and do whatever is necessary to bring an end to his harassment. I'll take the pictures / videos, and if he makes a scene, I'll have it out with him. I feel that this is the only approach to take. I'm 67 years old now at the time of this writing, and I simply can't continue to live with Maurice's BS any longer.

Also, since all this had happened to me, I have made several friends from anti-bully crusades who, I'm sure, will back me up with whatever I decide to do.

- CHAPTER FIVE -

My final days in Wexford

It's Friday evening, and while still in a total state of shock, I called my instructor at the Tang Soo Do Karate School I have been going to for over the last several months.

I was to be tested for my next rank on the following morning. In shape I was in, I was going to cancel, but he had talked me into being there at 9:00 am on that Saturday morning.

It's the next morning, and I went into the school. I then discussed my situation with some of my friends I had met there and then went through the 2-hour test with the rest of the class.

After that several of us it was agreed to meet over at Ziggy's, the local cigar bar around the corner of my apartment. This became a hangout of mine that one of my friends, Tom, had introduced me to.

Anyway, I met several friends there and had a wonderful time. Tom knew my situation and felt bad for me and what had happened, but still, we made the best of things.

Beauty from Pittsburgh

One evening a gorgeous woman came upstairs and introduced herself to me and asked if she could have a cigar. I said sure, and she had become very close and very friendly with me if you know what I mean. For the sake of argument, I'll name her Sue.

Sue came up to visit me several times, but I didn't try anything because she had once told me that she was engaged to the DJ who was working downstairs. She just liked to flirt while smoking my cigars.

Then one evening it happened. My friend Tom and Master "C" from our studio were all upstairs smoking cigars, and Sue walks into where we were sitting. This time she became very friendly towards me where she actually began to make out with me.

After a short while, I said to myself, "Let's see how far she wants to go". I began to slide my hand down her pants and then began to work my way around to her front.

Oh my God, I couldn't believe she was actually letting me do this. Then suddenly something came over me. I then immediately took my hand out because I suddenly had the idea that Maurice was somewhere in the restaurant, and he might have put her up to this to keep me occupied.

Maybe this girl is a hooker and Maurice had put her up to it to keep me occupied. I'm old, a little overweight, why the hell would any woman, especially someone as cute as her want to spend this kind of time with me?

I immediately got up, stood in the doorway and yelled to Tom that I think he's here. Tom said, "who Maurice?" I said "YES".

Tom then mentioned to our Karate master, who was sitting there smoking his cigar, that I think that the Bully was somewhere on the premises. So, the three of us went downstairs to look around and see if we can find him.

Being Blown Away

As if my story isn't amazing enough, the following takes the cake. It shows how someone can be a true manipulator with anyone he comes in contact with.

The three of us are at the bottom of the steps and I pear into the main room of the restaurant. I see Maurice sitting there and talking with a large group of people.

Master "C," told me specifically that I need to point at Maurice before he can take any action (getting physical). Tom looked at me with agreement of what he said.

So, I grasp enough courage to walk out there and face him and who did I see? Not only did I see Maurice, but I also saw the Sr. Director of HR, and my old boss from City Ward Financial, several of my old teammates, as well as the people from Mermaid Appliances (Maurice's friend and the Manager who was going to hire him).

The Director and Maurice were doing most of the talking and arguing with each other about what this bully had done to me. "You ruined the man's career" the Director was saying. Maurice said "yes, I know. That was my plan".

Maurice continued by telling everyone that he was lying about everything basically to get reactions out of you, and it worked. You did what I wanted you to do.

At this point, everyone there was in total shock. They just couldn't believe what they were hearing. They all then realized that I was standing there in total shock and filed with a lot of fear.

After Maurice sat there with one of his horrific looks at me, I just could NOT point at him. My finger was pointing up in the air but not at Maurice. All it took was just one look from him, and I could not move a muscle. I was frozen.

With everyone there in the room, Sue standing behind me smiling as if she's thinking that I'm going to do something, and my Tang Soo Do Master standing and chatting with my old boss. I was hit with so much fear I suddenly was unable to move at all.

God only knows why this had happened to me. If I only had pointed out my problems with this clown would have been over. Not only would my martial art friends have kicked the shit out of Maurice, but I would probably have been given my job back.

I will never forget that day for as long as I live. If I only could have been more assertive, not only on that day but especially when this whole story unfolded back in 2005 when he first began his reign of terror on me.

I'm coming forward with my story so that if you or anyone you know is being harassed and bullied in the work place, you MUST TAKE IMMEDIATE ACTION before it gets out of hand. And what's most important is that you will save your job or better yet move on to greener pastures.

March 31st 2013 came, and my good friend Tom helped me move my stuff out of my Wexford apartment, and I thanked him and drove back home a broken man.

- CHAPTER SIX -

What should I have done?

At Data Systems:

OK, thinking back, it's 2005 when this whole thing started with Maurice. My boss at Data Systems with the help of his Senior Architect of our department kept slipping everything he did to me under the rug.

What I should have done is to send private e-mails directly to HR. I should have begun an open dialogue with someone in that department. I should have sent emails to that HR person who came in from Havertown PA to interview the two of us.

I then could explain my specific situation with someone who would listen. During that period, Maurice has been contacting HR, himself, making it appear that I had done something wrong. At this time, I was somewhat intimidated by any corporate HR department in general.

My boss even told me to make a list of what Maurice was actually doing to me. He also made it a point to tell me to "don't send it in the form of an e- mail". Just jot it down in a personal log. Do NOT send it as an e-mail. Talk about covering his own ass!

I later discovered that all he was actually concerned about is that two-year severance package that Senior Management had offered him after I was gone.

I wonder how things would have happened if I only sent e-mails to HR and copying my boss and maybe that lead architect of his?

E-mailing or texting with a specific timestamp actually creates an audit trail which can be used as a form of proof that something (bullying) had actually happened. I then would have actual evidence that I could show to an employment lawyer.

I regret not taking the appropriate action with HR. I just couldn't believe my boss actually said to me about the e-mailing, but I still did what he had requested. I wrote a list which really looked as if I was paranoid.

The document sounded like something of which no one would ever make an effort to do to another person. The types of things that this bully had done to me were simply unheard of.

Whenever you are being bullied in the workplace, you must take immediate action and bring an end to such harassment before it's too late. NEVER Ignore the Bully. He/she will never go away unless you take immediate action. There are ways to get results peacefully and without any violence.

Whatever Maurice had said to others, specifically, about me that they were all lies, period.

Text messaging wasn't available back then but e-mailing sure was. I should have sent private e-mails to someone in HR. Especially that person who my boss actually brought in from Havertown, Pennsylvania, to interview myself, Maurice, and any witnesses who worked in the surrounding area.

Sending e-mails each time you're being bullied, explaining the situation when it happens actually creates an audit trail of such behavior, which could have been used as evidence. Whenever you're being bullied, you need to always remember to document everything. "Document! Document! Document!" as the saying goes.

I remember that HR person from Havertown being very sympathetic towards me. He seemed to be standing behind me, and I should have used him during this difficult period in my life.

If I kept communication open, I would have known that he was quietly replaced.

With everything that was going on, I should not have taken everything personally and stay on the defensive with that entire BS this bully had thrown at me. He has been a pathological liar whenever he had the chance with his continuing effort to defame my character.

When you don't speak up, you end up really getting the short end of the stick. You end up getting screwed over.

After I finally left Data Systems, I had no idea that this idiot actually kept tabs of me as I worked around the country. This absurd obsession with hurting me is really something which should be investigated. His goal was to destroy my career completely, and he succeeded in doing just that. Oh My God.

Visits in Little Rock (2009 - 2012)

I know this is very hard to believe, but after I left Data Systems and began working around the country as a consultant, I actually ran into him. No, actually he deliberately ran into me!

The place was Little Rock Arkansas, and the company where I worked had its share of dirty politics and bullies. When you worked as a consultant, most of the managers wouldn't even talk to you, directly, unless you were an employee.

My new manager had a reputation of being a bully himself, playing favorites. After the eight-month contract had ended, I was hired as a full-time employee, and after that, things changed. Around three days after I was hired, three individual co-workers came over and warned me about something.

They each told me that my new manager, Jason, "likes to play favorites, and I am definitely not one of them". Long story short, I had a new bully to worry about in the workplace.

Over the four years I was there, Jason belittled me in front of others at meetings, and wherever he could, such as Christmas parties, and other team outings.

Since my story is not really about him, I'm not going to dwell on his behavior other than saying that I should have contacted the ethics department of HR about him, documenting everything he was doing to me and requesting to be transferred to the other manager that worked there. She was fair, and we respected each other, which is how it should be in any company where you work.

Basically, I not only had to deal with the visits from Maurice but also had to put up with all of Jason's bull shit as well.

When I went out to lunch with my co-workers, I would always bring up some of the stuff that Maurice did to me at my old company. I constantly had that crap on my mind while I was doing my new job. I later realized that this behavior was due to the fact that I was really suffering from PTSD.

Maurice made his unannounced visits, and I would literally shut him off and pretend that I didn't really see anything. I don't know exactly what the hell Maurice had done to me but my God, the fear I get from him every time I so much as think of that horrible bully is really amazing.

I should have notified the police as soon as I first saw him in Little Rock standing in front of that garage next to where I parked my car.

I should have been able to put two and two together and had a major investigation done after I first discovered my car damaged that day in my parking lot where I had lived.

But I didn't. Instead, I froze up with all kinds of fear with what I know that man is really capable of and who had harassed and tormented me all these years.

Also, several people had advised me that it looked like a utility truck had hit my car; I never stopped to think that Maurice just may have been the real culprit.

It's truly amazing just how this fear I have of Maurice can overwhelm me to the point where I don't even consider him a possibility as to the cause. This idea just never entered my mind.

Now let's also assume that Maurice had somehow contacted Jason. I only mention this because in 2012 Jason had set me up to be part of that big layoff where I was laid off on July 20, 2012.

If I had contacted the Ethics department of HR like I was supposed to about Jason, I probably would still be working there. But I didn't, I was laid off and that small severance I received paid for my move back to my home in Pennsylvania. I left Little Rock on September 30 2012 and was very excited about my new contract which I would be starting in the following October 15th.

Visits in Pittsburgh (October 15, 2012 – January 25, 2013)

What had happened to me in Pittsburgh, PA is truly unbelievable. I was working as a consultant for 90 days, of which if they liked what I was doing, they would offer me a very lucrative full-time position.

Now being a consultant, you really need to be careful. That said, there are still things I could have done without getting in trouble or being suddenly terminated.

Since my new boss had told me that I was doing a great job, I thought that everything was going well and I had a great chance of being offered a full- time position. I was so wrong.

The closest thing to documenting everything is what I'm stating in this book. I made the huge mistake of not documenting anything and keeping quiet.

As soon as I saw that idiot on the campus, I should have spoken up. When he first walked across the driveway, in front of my car, towards the entrance of building four of the complex, I should have taken the appropriate steps to put an end of his evil plans to get me fired.

With that one security guard stepping outside, giving me dirty looks while standing next to Maurice, I should have insisted on speaking to his supervisor.

When I ran into my boss talking to the Director of HR, rather than not speaking up, I should have immediately requested a meeting with him and my boss.

Because of the fact that I kept quiet, I lost my job. Whenever he said negative things (lies) about me, I should have spoken up and explained to everyone what this man really is. He's a very horrible bully plain and simple.

Keeping quiet became my downfall. I should have instead gone to that manager who was interviewing Maurice for a position with our neighboring company; I should have made it a point to speak to him.

I also should have contacted the HR department of the company where the IT team worked and which was escorting Maurice around the campus.

Again, since I didn't properly document all this harassing activity that Maurice had done to me, that my hands were tied after I was let go. I couldn't do anything because it was his word against mine. If I tried suing, I would most likely have lost.

The only evidence is the fact that Maurice had signed in at the front security desk each time he was on campus. He signed there many times while I was there.

Since my boss stopped me when I was about to go outside and confront him when he disrupted our meeting on the first floor, I should have stepped back and made some plans of my own to talk to those who escorted him into and out of the building.

But I didn't. When my boss had told me that I was doing a great job, I never thought that this clown could do so much to hurt me the way that he did.

When I was let go on that Friday, I was totally devastated. I just could NOT believe what had happened. I was in total shock. No one at any company had talked to me at all about with what this idiot had said to them which got them to suddenly have my contract terminated.

When I discussed the sudden decision with my boss, his reasoning was so far absurd as with this bully got away with doing to me.

- CHAPTER SEVEN -

Helping out where I can

My Anti-Bully app available for android and I-Phone app Stores:

Not to blow my own horn, but in 2014, I actually created an anti-bully app which can be used to create such audit trails I mentioned earlier. The app designed for Android and the iPhone can be used to document bullied assaults with exact timestamps of which I feel can be used in a court of law.

The name of the app is Bully Proof Assistant. I have both free and paid versions available on each platform.

Now when you first look at them, you will notice that it's been a while since they were last updated. So, that said, please note that I am making major changes to these apps which should become available in the near future. Here is a pic of my latest iPhone version:

My android version is very similar. One of my changes will be to bring both of these apps in sync with the same functionality.

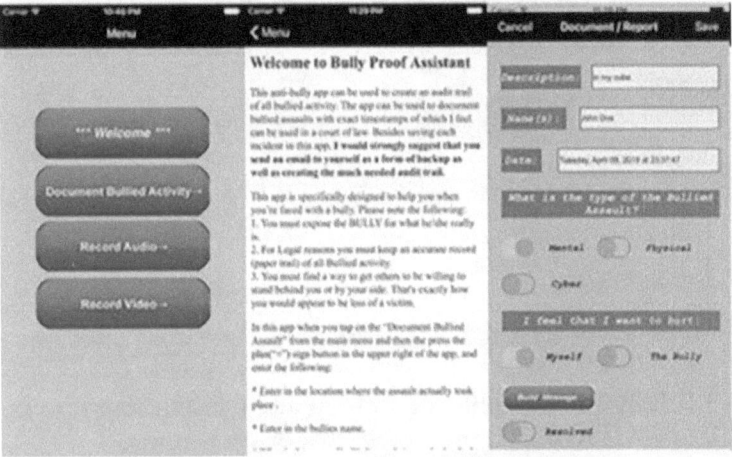

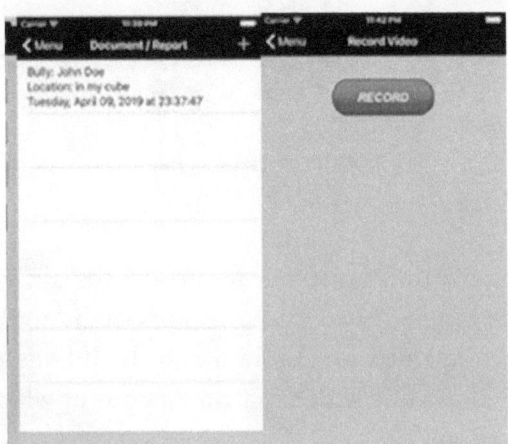

I wish I had this tool available to me back in 2005 because I could have gone somewhere where I could have some privacy and send an e-mail to that HR guy from Havertown. At the time, the only places

I knew of where I could have some privacy was in the bathroom stall or at home.

The bully was so far up my ass I needed to be as discreet as possible. As I mentioned before, it was as if the main job of Maurice was to aggressively bully me all day long.

I know what it feels like when you're being bullied. I know that when you're targeted by someone, you have feelings of confusion, anger, not sure who to turn to, low self-confidence, and probably some low self-esteem.

When you run into this type of situation, as I mentioned before, you need to bring a swift end to such harassment.

This app is specifically designed to help you when you're faced with such a dilemma. Please note the following:

You must expose the BULLY for what he/she really is.

For Legal reasons, you must keep an accurate record (paper trail) or Bullied activity.

You must find a way to get others to be willing to stand behind you your side. That's exactly how you would appear to be less of a victim.

In this app when you tap on the "Document Bullied Assault" from the main menu and then the press the plus ("+") sign button in the upper right of the app, enter in the bully's name and where the assault took place (location), and then answer the following selected questions:

What is the type of bullied assault (mental, physical, cyber)?

I feel I want to hurt (myself, the bully)?

After that, press enter the "Incident Report" (soon being changed to "Build Message") button, and an emergency report is built and ready to be sent out to anyone who can come to your aid for help and support.

Also, if in the event you and the bully resolve things on your own, you can mark the bullied incident as resolved and e-mail all those who received an original message from you stating that you and the person who had bullied had resolved the issue amongst yourselves.

The app also has functionality to record voice or create a video of the incident. The voice recordings are saved onto a list just like the "Document Bullied Assault" is. The video is saved on your phone in the video library.

This is good practice where the app will generate an emergency email for you.

You can send this message to HR person or anyone on your team who can help you during this difficult time. I would even send the email to myself as a form of backup which you can save.

Saving messages about such bullying, is a great way to keep an audit trail that such harassment had taken place. An accurate timestamp is also saved in a list within the app.

Eliminating such horrifying harassment at work (office jerk or in school will also eliminate much of the unnecessary stress in your life. As difficult as it may be, you must address the situation before it's too late. Just remember you are not alone.

This anti-bullying app is designed to be used by anyone who is being targeted and bullied in the playground or the workplace. Currently, with the Android version of the app, a special "settings" option has been added to the menu selection. All you need to do is check off the environment where you are being Bullied (playground or workplace). The app will use that selection to generate an appropriate message to be sent out. This app is also useful for someone who is targeted on the internet (cyber bullies), and if you, the target, are having thoughts of harming yourself or the bully.

My main goal is to use the latest technology available to combat all forms of Bullying as peacefully as possible. I also would like to hear from anyone who has been bullied in the workplace.

Bully Proof Assistant Professional works fine on the phone or tablet for any living environment and for any age. I'm hoping that people who are being targeted by bullies will try this app and give me their opinion of the app.

If there are any issues, or suggestions for the app, please let me know, and I will immediately look into it. I am currently working on making several enhancements, and I will definitely look at your suggestions.

Also, please feel free to check out my web site: www.bullyproofnetwork.org. I also have a page on Facebook.

If you like what I'm doing, please let me know. I would love to hear from you. We all need to work together to make our world a better place to live.

- CHAPTER EIGHT -

A New and Promising Future

Our Anti-Bully Crusade

A couple of years ago, I started my organization, changing the name from Bully Proof Assistant to the Bully Proof Network (www.bullyproofnetwork.org). The idea around this is to build a network of people who can come to the immediate aid for help and support of anyone who is being bullied, either at work or in our schools. God willing, this will eventually become a non-profit organization.

As I said before, I don't ever want what had happened to me to ever happen to anyone else. Each day my voice is being heard from people who have been supporting me over the years.

As mentioned in the previous chapter, I designed, developed, and implemented an anti-bully app for the Android and I-Phone cell phones. Later in 2019, I plan to make several more upgrades to both versions of these apps. The links to the apps is as follows:

I-Phone: https://itunes.apple.com/us/app/bullyproofassistant-documents/id1069679369?ls=1&mt=8 – free with ads https://itunes.apple.com/us/app/bully-proof-assistant-prof/id1115440058? ls=1&mt=8 – paid (99 cents)

I also have an android version of the Bully Proof Assistant app available on the google play App Store and is currently in the process of being revised to give the same look and feel as the above I-phone versions. This new version should be available in a couple of months.

Our anti-bully campaign has been growing in leaps and bounds over the years. This is a great thing and you're all invited to join us.

Today I am making several enhancements to these apps for both the Android and the I-phone. I'm bringing the best of both versions of my apps available on both platforms.

In fact, I actually outsourced the maintenance of these apps to programmers who can assist me in getting the changes done promptly.

Seems a little strange considering that it's been over ten years since my position at Data Systems has been outsourcing to India, and now I am doing some outsourcing myself. Ha-ha.

I also have been giving free help and support to those who have been suffering from bullying in the workplace. Every one of them had greatly appreciated the help and support I have given them over the years.

Living on Social's Security's Early Retirement program has not been an easy task for me. So, a few months ago, I have been investigating several popular online affiliate programs where I could earn a little extra income. Well, they didn't really pan out very well.

Currently, I work part-time, testing web sites and phone apps with my devices.

I am also planning to create some new phone apps to keep myself involved with programming, which I love to do.

I also go to the Gym, where I'm taking Tai Chi, and taking Kenpo Karate here in Florida where I am currently living and moving forward with my life.

The bottom line to my story is this. If you ever find yourself being bullied in your workplace, you must nip it in the bud immediately. If you don't, you could find yourself in the unemployment line, regardless as to how well you are really performing in your job.

I realize that I was not the only victim here in my story. Each of those large and successful corporations I mentioned, as well as their employees and managers who had witnessed all the bullying performed by Maurice, were all victims as well.

Please note that I forgive every one of you who had mistreated me where I had worked. If you want, you can always get in touch with me on Facebook at https://www.facebook.com/bobsbullyproofnetwork/ or on my new web site: www.bullyproofnetwork.org.

- CHAPTER NINE -

The real question is WHY?

This chapter identifies two possible theories as to why Maurice would possibly want to continue with his reign of terror on me.

The first possibility is ego. This man had taken whatever reputation I had at Data Systems and completely destroyed it to the point where when the programs which I was responsible for had been outsourced to India, that I had to be the person in the company to be let go. Not Him.

After I left in August 2007, Maurice had taken over my position, and I was let go, even though I had spent ten years of my life working on all that software. After all those lies and BS that Maurice had said to my co-workers, which were on my teams as well as all the levels of management, that I had to be the person to be let go.

While I was training those people from India, I applied for several other positions that the company had. I actually thought that I had a chance until I overheard one of the VP's in my area, stating that I needed to be let go.

I don't know what Maurice had told others about me, but they must have been some horrendous lies. No one within the company would give me the time of day, let alone hire me in their department.

In their eyes, I had to be the one let go. So, on August 31 2007, I was the one laid off.

While I was sitting at home, I was getting calls from several head hunters, and finally, after a couple of months, I began accepting consulting gigs around the country.

After I landed my first position in Austin, Texas, a couple of friends had told me that Maurice actually knew where I was working. That he was very funny with joking around at meetings about me and that he knew where I was working.

Ok, so he was tracking me. At that time, I didn't think much of it. I didn't see him in Texas or Eden Prairie, Minnesota.

It wasn't until I had worked for over a year in Little Rock, Arkansas when I noticed him on that one day while I was walking to my car after work.

I think it was his ego, which led him to Arkansas. He knew people there because every time I saw him, he was being chauffeured around with a group of people.

Who the hell are these people? What lies has he told them about me? I will probably never know.

So, his ego takes over, and since I'm not working at Data Systems any more, he likes the idea of harassing me whenever he gets a chance regardless as to where I am living and working.

What makes my story more amazing is that it appears that he is only harassing me. That I'm the only one he bullies. When others, who know him, talk about him, I only hear good things about him. In their eyes, he's a really nice guy.

But as I said before, if you put us both in the same room, he immediately acts like he's going to get violent. He makes all kinds of dirty looks as if I had done something very wrong.

The second possibility as to why he continues to harass me is this. Remember when Maurice had discussed with me just who he really was while we were walking in the park?

This is around three months before he began his reign of terror on me back in 2005. That he has something on one of the Senior Managers there at Data Systems, now I most likely will never know as to what that is, but it does make me wonder.

Could this senior manager be doing something illegal whereas some code was added within my programs to add money from transactions into a secret account? If this was the case than Maurice's constant barrage of harassment actually makes sense.

This would be a good reason to get me out of the picture by making me somewhat crazy to the point where my career was completely ruined.

At this point, I just want to say that if God forbid, something was to ever happen to me, that there should be an investigation done with all those involved.

Check with the number of times that bully signed in at the security desk in building Four where I had worked in Warrendale Pennsylvania.

Follow the money and any activity on PC's, phones, etc. How's Maurice keeping track of me? Good question. I believe it's from my social media accounts.

Just remember that all names used here in this book are fictitious. So, make sure you get the right names when doing your research.

- CHAPTER TEN -

Grace and Forgiveness

This chapter describes what some friends at my church had told me that I need to do to give me the strength I need to move forward with my life. That said, as religious as I feel I am, I found this technique extremely difficult for me to do.

- Whenever I discuss to others as to what Maurice had done to me, I explain to them that I feel that he created a hole in my soul.
- If anyone reading this feels that discussing a little religion will make you feel uncomfortable, feel free to move on to the next chapter.
- If there is any reason as to why I should be angry with anyone, and would ever want to go, Postal, Maurice definitely fits the bill. Let's take a closer look as to what damage all this constant barrage of harassment from him has really cost me:
- Post-Traumatic Stress Disorder. I was first diagnosed with this back in 2 Co-pays at a weekly / monthly Doctor's visits had added up over the year. In August 2006 I had a major flair-up with Regional Enteritis (inflammation of the small intestines) to the point where I had my second bowel resection surgery. The

inflammation that caused a blockage and the beginning stages of peritonitis is known to be caused by excessive stress.
- I was out of the office for a total of eight months. Six of those months due to a muscle seizure I had after my bowel resection surgery. Neurologist had to take away my driver's license temporarily.
- Poor reputation where ever this bully has been. Data Systems, Mer Appliances, City Ward Financial, and where I worked and lived in Rock, Arkansas.
- Due to what the bully has gotten away with, I had problems with gritting teeth every time I thought of the types of things this bully did. That ruined my front two bridges in my mouth.
- In fact, one evening while I was home in Wexford, I had pushed on my front bridge to the point where the upper right side had busted out. I kept it glued together with Pollutant until I could get to the dentist.
- Today both of these bridges are being replaced with a new Partial. I'm using a temporary bridge today while I'm working on this book.
- Lost position as a developer with Data Systems after over Ten years honorable service (1997 – 2007). I lost another position at City Financial as a Tandem Consultant (2012 – 2013).
- Bankruptcy chapter 7 completed in September 2017. I now find myself in worst financial situation I've ever been to.
- Our home in Pennsylvania has been foreclosed. I wasn't able to pay mortgage since February 2013. We lost the home in October 2017.
- Early Retirement: Since I couldn't find a new position after City Financial, I took early retirement with the Social Security Administration soon as I turned age 62. Because I did this, I am collecting a lot less these than I would have been getting if I could have waited until I turned age 65.

After all these, it's really amazing that I didn't go postal. My minister and others at my church had told me a new philosophy for me to work on. When I first heard of this, I couldn't believe what they were saying.

My first reaction was asking them if they knew what this guy actually had done to me. He basically had recked havoc with my life and ruined my perfectly good career. Did you read what I had on my web site www.bullyproofassistant.com and www.bullyproofnetwork.org

They all said yes. They said, "You need to work on forgiving Maurice for what he had done to you."

I asked how? They said, "pray to our Lord that he will give you direction on how to do this. " The concept is that you turn all your judgments over to our Lord God. You are forgiving him for what he had done to you and allowing our Lord God to judge him fairly and punish him accordingly.

I don't really know what he had done to me, but I have an extreme fear of Maurice. Whenever I see him, I freeze up with a lot of fear of him and immediately work at ignoring his presence as much as possible. When I do that, it makes it easier for him to work his harassment technics on me and what's worse, he gets away with it.

Now, as I look back at all this harassment that he had done to me, I realize that the more that I ignore him and run away in the other direction, the more aggressive he gets with his controlling harassment techniques on me.

But then, after several years, I had a real epiphany on what I really need to do in order for me to heal and finally go on with my life.

Currently, I can't actually forgive Maurice for what he had done to me, but what I can do is give forgiveness to myself for allowing myself to let Maurice bully me in the horrific way that he did.

Then, eventually, I may be able to forgive Maurice for what he had done.

At the time of this writing, head hunters continue to call me for assignments around the country.

I feel that if I was hired again, there is an excellent possibility that I would see Maurice again. If or when that happens, I realize that I must also be much more assertive and focus on gathering whatever evidence I can to put an end to this whole thing. Regardless as to worrying about being terminated from another contract, I need to get some immediate assistance and try to prevent it while at the same time concentrate on keeping in control and demonstrate forgiveness. Forgiveness, in a sense, that I must simply turn everything that is being done to me over to our Lord God.

The best option for me is turning all my feelings over and allow our Lord to judge him as he will judge me. I honestly feel that our Lord will judge him some time and punish him accordingly.

I've been praying for this for quite a while now, and I find myself feeling a lot less depressed and angry over what had happened to me all these years.

But every once in a while, I think of some of the things of what this guy had actually done to me and those horrible feelings I mentioned earlier, come back to the surface. When that happens, I step back and work at looking at my situation a little more objectively, begin some praying, and those feelings dissipate away.

The following is taken from the last pages of the book "Grace and Forgiveness" by John and Carol Arnott:

"A prayer to break the bondage of judgments over those who hurt us."

"John 10:10 says the enemy is a thief who comes to steal, kills, and destroys. But Jesus has broken the power of the enemy and overwritten that curse of death with His own life. In the same verse, he affirms, "I have come that you might have life and have it more abundantly".

"This means that we need to take a giant step into the Grace of God and stop living a life limited by the bondage of judgments."

"After having prayed a prayer of forgiveness for those who have hurt you, and having repented of judging them, pray the following prayer of release. Rise in your authority as a believer and free yourself from these situations!"

"Father, in the name of Jesus I cut myself free from every soulish, ungodly tie to every person who has sinned against me, who has ever hurt me, who has abused me either emotionally or physically in any way. I sever those unholy ties now in the name of Jesus, and I free myself from their control."

"Father, I free myself from every bit of demonic oppression that has come to me down the generational stream of my family. Thank you that the blood of Jesus Christ, God's son, frees me from control, witchcraft, fear, violence, shame, abuse, and pain. There is now no condemnation for me as I am in Christ, Jesus. Not because I deserve that, Lord, but because it is a gift to me from you. It has all been paid for by your Son, Jesus. Thank You, Lord."

"I step forward now and take hold of the freedom you have won for me, Lord Jesus. I receive the Grace of God. Thank you that this is part of my inheritance in Christ. I affirm my identity in your Son Jesus, and I thank you that I am a new creation in him. The law of the spirit of life in Christ Jesus has set me free from the law of sin and death. I take my freedom!" (Romans 8:2)

It's November 2016 and by a strange coincidence that a good friend of mine gave me a copy of an article about this very subject. What's strange about it is that it was just before I had decided to make updates to this book.

"Sunday, November 6, Luke 6:20:31, All Saints Sunday – Pray for those who abuse you. (v. 28)

"Not everyone has been a saint to me, and while praying for my enemies is hard, praying for those who abuse me has proven extremely difficult. With enemies, there is often a sense of respect, but my abusers have no respect for me at all. I mean nothing to them, maybe even less than nothing. They denigrate, destroy, and do all under a twisted veneer of caring and compassion. And they are the ones whom I'm supposed to pray? Yikes. But there it is, right in the Bible."

"I did it. I prayed for my abusers. And a funny thing happened. The more I prayed for my abusers, the more at peace I became with what they had done. It became easier to move on. Somehow, by praying for them, what they had done hurt less. Weird, right?"

"I don't think God put this verse in the bible for our abusers. God put it there for those of us who have been abused. Praying for our abusers is not a way for them to heal; it's a way for us to heal. Praying for our abusers is a gift we give to ourselves, one that is difficult to unwrap but is definitely worth the effort."

"God of all help me pray for those who have hurt me the worst. In Christ's name Amen."

You see, I'm not just praying for Maurice, who began his reign of terror on me way back when we both worked at Data Systems Corporation in Delaware and has continued to wreak havoc with my life for several years after I had left.

I'm praying for the Senior Director, my old Manager, and colleagues at City Ward Financial who listened to the filthy lies and just took the easy way out by terminating my contract there in January 2013.

I'm praying for the young overweight security guard and the older woman from Mermaid Appliances who greeted me each morning at the front security desk in Building 4 of the complex where I had once worked. They listened and believed in all the filthy lies and rumors Maurice had said to them. Maurice is a real manipulator and is very convincing, and it's not your fault that you had to put up with all his shenanigans.

I'm also praying for my old Managers and colleagues at Data Systems Corporation who did not really understand what Maurice was doing to them, the department, and to me with his evil plan.

I am praying for all of you with continued good fortune for you and your families. In Jesus name, Amen.

I am very curious as to what Maurice actually told the Mermaid Appliances Security Guards and the manager who had escorted him in and out of building #4.

I'm aware that the manager who did that just wanted to see what the bully was really capable of and regretted as to what had happened to me. Everyone who was there during that time was all victims to the antics of this very horrible Bully.

All that said, there's no going back. What had happened, happened.

We can all learn from this and, hopefully, this sort of thing will never happen to anyone again.

One final note in this chapter is this. The Jesus Creed is something we have been reciting at church, which is what we believe Jesus would want us to do. I even created a free app for the I-Phone, which displays this very verse.

DAVID GIDEON

<u>The Jesus Creed (Mark 12:29-31):</u>

"Hear O Israel
The Lord our God,
The Lord is One;
You shall love the Lord your God With all your heart,
and with all your soul,
and with all your mind,
and with all your strength.

The second is this,
You shall love your neighbor as yourself.
There is no other Commandment greater than these."

PART TWO

Advice and Support – This part will focus on some suggestions for you to get the advice and support you need when you're assaulted by bullies.

SECTION I - LEGAL ACTION

1. Document every bullied assault. Note the date and time of each incident best method is by sending out an e-mail or text message to someone where they come to your immediate aid for help and support.
As a backup, you must remember to at least send the email to yourself. This is not only a form of backup but is also creating an audit trail of such bullied activity.
2. Learn the anti-bully laws in the state where you are working. Employ laws against bullying are being passed on a state-by-state basis. An excellent web site to learn what laws are available in your state is at: https://healthyworkplacebill.org/states/.
3. Contact HR and find out how they can help. Find someone there who you can confide in and get information as to how they can help you. Every company has its own set of ethic policies. It's best to find out what those policies and how you can best benefit from them.
4. If things are getting tough at work, remember to gather your document (proof) of every bullied incident, and set up an appointment with employment attorney as soon as possible. You need to discuss your special issues with someone who can give you some sound advice and what options are. I would strongly suggest that you don't let anyone at work know that you sought legal advice until it's absolutely necessary.

5. If things get really tough with the bully, you will have to plan on confront the situation head-on. Work on controlling yourself and

don't allow them to bring yourself down to his/her level. Avoid violence wherever possible.
6. If he gets physical, do not reciprocate, or you will most likely get fired. You need to focus on proving that the bully is the person who is in the wrong. You have to work on exposing the bully for what he/she really is.
7. At this point, you already should have been discussing your situation with the employment attorney. You might be able to take legal action against company. This will be the hardest thing that you will ever have to do you'll be respected a lot more if you stand up for yourself.

SECTION II

Should and Should Not
In the Workplace - What Should the Witnesses Do?

With my personal experience with everything I went through, I feel that I can shed a little light as to what someone should do in the event, they witness someone in your office who is bullying someone else.

1. Stay alert while in the office. Remember that the bully is real manipulator. He likes an audience, and everyone is a puppet where he will pull as many strings as he/she can. When you see someone being bullied, you should stand behind and support the Target during the assault. Never bully.
2. If the bully schedules an event and deliberately works on disassociating the target with the rest of the group by not inviting him/her in any social activities such as lunch or a golf outing, publically invite his/her victim, will help with keeping the sanity in the office and show the bully that everybody is going to play the game his / her way.
3. If the Manager is the bully and the victim (target) is being bullied severely by others in the department should come forward and show support for target.

Look at it this way; he's not going to fire everybody. There's always power in the masses and the power of the bully will eventually, weaken as his audience dissipates.

In the Work Place - What Should You (The Target) Focus On

The target (victim) should understand that he/she is not alone. Bullies are themselves cowards who work on getting ahead by beating up on someone he/she considers to be weak.

Besides reviewing all of the legal suggestions in section, I include the following:

1. Don't ever take anything personally. It's easy to blame yourself but don't The bully who has targeted me is a real expert at making all kinds of nasty looks at his target (me), which made me feel like I did something horribly wrong.

    An expert bully is a real terrorist who strives to play all sorts of head games in an effort to knock down your self-confidence and self-esteem.

    I made the mistake of going on the defensive and taking things personally. All that did was giving the bully more power over me, which lowered my self-esteem and self-confidence. In my case, they both went to an all-time low.

2. If your being Bullied, and he acts like he's going to get more aggressive start a fight, leave immediately and go straight to your Manager. If he/s not available or appears to cover up the bully's mayhem, go straight to and if that person isn't any help to you, visit the Senior HR person and it a point not to leave that office until you feel satisfied.

    Don't worry about being fired. If no action is taken, you may have a lawsuit brewing in your favor.

3. I know this is hard, but do your best not to be intimidated. The person was bullying me was very intimidating. He intimidated me and acted everyone else best friend at the same time. This blew away everyone o team and eventually separated me from the rest of the team. I was the p that had to leave the company. Not the bully.

4. If things get really tough with the bully, you will have to plan on confront the situation head-on. Just make sure you don't get violent.

   If he gets physical, do not reciprocate, or you will most likely get fired. Make sure that you thoroughly document everything and work on proving that the bully is the person who is in the wrong. You have to work on exposing the bully for what he/she really is.

5. Don't keep obsessing about what the bully had done in the past. This huge mistake I made. After I left Data Systems, while working around country as a consultant, I kept obsessing about what that very horrible had done to me.

   Sure, I got a little sympathy, but in hind sight, I realize that this was a huge mistake. What you're actually doing is showing your weakness side and how vulnerable you can get.

6. Don't ever assume that things will ever get better. This was another mistake I made.

   Whenever that idiot was bullying me, I focused on ignoring him wherever and whenever I could. I should have confronted the situation head-on by being more assertive and focusing on what the bully was actually doing.

7. When working in your desired profession, work at your hardest to keep great reputation. If it becomes tarnished in any way, focus on cleaning it Bullies look for their target by finding someone who might be considered the weakest link in the group or department.

8. If you see secret meetings going on, get assertive immediately and in yourself to the meetings and don't ever take NO for an answer.

   I saw this happen while performing my last job in Pittsburgh, PA. I was told to stop attending weekly staff meetings, and when the security guard wanted to have a private meeting with my boss, I should have been much more assertive.

But I wasn't. Instead, I was terminated because of this inaction.

9. If you think you need help, you probably do. Don't be afraid, be assertive and get the help from HR or whoever is available in your company or surrounding area to immediately give you the help you need. It's important, however, that when talking to HR or management to remain calm and matter of fact so that you don't appear like chicken little crying that the sky is falling.

Remember to have respect for yourself and think of yourself as being number one.

10. If the bully is deliberately excluding you from an outing (lunch, twilight etc.), be brave and deliberately invite yourself. What could the bully do? Someone on the team would most likely welcome you.

In School - What Should the Witnesses Do

When I was a youngster, I was bullied by other kids, some of whom were older than me. The bullying was done, usually with a group of onlookers. With my personal experience with everything I went through, I feel that I can shed a little light as to what someone should do in the event you as a child, witness someone being bullied.

1. Remember that the bully is really a manipulator. He/she likes an audience and everyone is a puppet where he/she will pull as many strings as he can. When you see someone being bullied, you should stand behind victim and show support during the assault.

2. Don't be afraid to report the incident to someone who can come to the person who you see is being bullied. The bully expects you to turn and ignore the situation. Muster the courage and do what's right.

3. Even if the teacher is the bully and the victim (target) is being bullied severely, others in the class should come forward and show support for the victim (target). Look at it this way; what is he/she going to do, fail the entire class? There's always power in the masses.

In School - What Should You (The Target) Focus On

Before I continue, I want to give you two definitions:

-Self-Confidence: *faith in one's own judgment, ability, etc.*
-Self-Esteem: *pride in one-self, self-respect.*

If a bully is victimizing you, you should understand that you are not the only person who is bullied. Bullies are themselves cowards who work on getting ahead by beating up on his/her target.

The real question is, why are you being targeted from bullies in the first place? Do you have a use-me abuse-me note taped across your forehead? Is there any information you can get on the internet or in books that can help you in taking preventive steps so that you're not targeted?

1. What you need to do is take up an activity or sport which can build high confidence and self-esteem. Taking karate or some other martial art is excellent choice. I've seen children who train in the martial arts, and they seem to have higher self-confidence and self- esteem than those who don't.
2. When you're targeted by a bully, the most important thing you need is to make sure you thoroughly document all bullied assaults. You are not just telling when you document in the form but you are actually sending an e-mail message to someone who can come to your aid for help and support.

In School, it could be your favorite teacher, guidance counselor, or other bystanders, who are also known to be your friends. You need to focus on getting people to stand behind you instead of the bully.

3. Don't be afraid to tell others as to what you're really feeling. Doing so may save your life. After my last assault, I must admit I have had though suicide or going postal on the bully who did me such harm.

   My Post Traumatic Stress Disorder was at an all-time high, and several years later, at the time of this re-writing, I am still being treated for it.

   If you're having such horrible thoughts, you have to muster the courage to let others know your true feelings. As I said before, you don't want to do anything that you will regret later.

4. Don't ever take anything personally. The bully who has targeted me was a real expert at making all kinds of nasty looks at his target, which makes feel like you did something horribly wrong.

   I made the mistake of going on the defensive and taking things personally. All that did was giving the bully more power over me, and it lowered my self- esteem and self-confidence. In my case they both went to an all-time low.

5. If your being bullied, and he acts like he's going to get more aggressive or start a fight with you, leave immediately and go straight to someone who stand behind you instead of the bully.

SECTION III

Some Anti-Bully Websites for help and support in the Workplace

Educate yourself with as much information as possible on the subject of bullying. The following list is the more popular ones I found on the internet. You need to get as much help and support as possible.

1. Great article on how to deal with a bully at http://humanresources.about.com/od/difficultpeople/ qt/work_bully.htm
2. Another great article on what not to do when your being bullied at work https://toughnickel.com/business/When-You-Are-Bullied-At-Work
3. Bully Proof Network (https://bullyproofnetwork.org) – this is my personal web site for my new non-profit 501c3 organization, where I will continue adding resources to help those who are victimized by bullies. As I discussed earlier, I have designed, developed, and published anti-bully apps for Android and I-phone. They are available on Google Play and the Apple I-tunes app store. The apps are designed to keep an accurate record of all bullied assaults. After a few clicks, the user can send out an emergency message to someone who can assist someone who is victimized by bullies (Bully Proof Assistant: for I-Phone, for Android).
4. Get a copy of The Bully At Work by Doctor's Gary and Ruth Namie excellent book on the subject of Work Place Bullying http://www.workplacebullying.org/individuals/ solutions/the-bully-at-work/

5. Search for anti-bully organizations on social networks such www.facebook.com, www.twitter.com, www.Linkedin.com

For Children:

Gather as much information as possible on the subject of bullying. The following list is the more popular ones on the internet for children. You need to get as much help and support as possible as soon as possible.

1. I'm Bully Free-The following is their **Mission Statement**:
   "I'm Bully Free's mission is to be a Center of Excellence and provide support and raise awareness to schools that have declared a commitment to creating and maintaining a **Bully-Free, Safe and Secure environment.** I'm Bully Free has schools, universities, corporations, and supporters around the world! Our stakeholders include schools, students, teachers and community members that work together to ensure that everyone feels respected, safe, and valued. Is your child being BULLIED by another student or staff member? Is the School District helping the situation? We can help! Call us at 713-478-3049. We will help! "http:// www.imbullyfree.org

2. The George Lucas Educational Foundation-This section has several articles on bullying prevention. "Explore how parents, educators, students, communities can work together to address the causes and effects of bullying and cyberbullying.": http:// www.edutopia.org/blogs/tag/bullying-prevention

3. StopBullying.gov provides information from various government agencies what bullying is, what cyberbullying is, who is at risk, and how you prevent and respond to bullying. http://www.Stopbullying.gov

4. John Anderson at Silvermanslim, a place where victims of stalking, a bullying, cyberbullying and other approved organizations can all together and help give support. A free website dedicated to victims of Bullying worldwide. All profiles and members who join re-checked validity and to ensure the safety of our members. Making other organizations know who to trust and what other

organizations to trust is our goal, uniting any trusted organizations under our wings. A compelling list of great organizations we feel are in the loop and do well for our children and teens. Organizations against abuse and bullying both in the community as well as online: https://silvermanslim.com

5. PACERS National Prevention Center – "Founded in 2006, PAC National Bullying Prevention Center actively leads social change, so bullying is no longer considered an accepted childhood rite of passage. PACER provides innovative resources for students, parents, educators, others, and recognizes bullying as a serious community issue that impedes education, physical and emotional health, and the safety and well-being of students. PACER offers digital-based resources for parents, schools, and youth": http://www.pacer.org/bullying/ There are new anti-bully organizations being created each day. To check the latest groups available and best fit for your situation, search for anti- organizations on social networks such as www.facebook, www.twitter.com, www.linkedin.com.

www.ingramcontent.com/pod-product-compliance
Lightning Source LLC
LaVergne TN
LVHW091557060526
838200LV00036B/880